Passive Income Strategies for Financial
Independence

Daniel Njuguna

DEDICATION

May this book serve as a beacon of hope for everyone who aspires to financial independence by showing them how to attain it through passive income. We are all inspired by your unwavering commitment to creating a more promising financial future.

Contents

Acknowledgments

With numerous people and resources' help, inspiration, and contributions, writing a book about Passive Income Strategies for Financial Independence is feasible. I want to thank everyone who has significantly helped make this endeavor a reality.

We express our sincere gratitude to:

- My loved ones, especially my family, for their unfailing encouragement and patience while I spent many hours reading, writing, and editing.

- The mentors who have shared their wisdom with us and guided us, igniting our desire for self-improvement and tenacity.

- The readers who joined us on our adventure searching for knowledge and inspiration to improve their lives.

- The book's editors, proofreaders, and publishing experts, whose skills turned our words into a polished and well-organized work.

We incredibly appreciate your generosity, which helped make this book possible. We hope the information contained within these pages will provide direction and empowerment for everyone on their financial independence journey.

Sincere appreciation,

DanielNjuguna

Introduction

Chapter 1: The Path to Financial Independence

1.1: Defining Financial Independence

Understanding the Concept

Financial independence (FI) is the condition in which your wealth and passive income sources are sufficient to pay your living expenses, allowing you to maintain your lifestyle without relying on traditional employment income. It is the capacity to direct your financial destiny and make decisions based on your values and ambitions rather than financial needs.

The Distinction from Retirement

Traditional retirement should not be confused with financial freedom. While retirement traditionally means a stoppage of work, financial independence allows you to choose whether or not to work, and it will enable you to pursue a career that coincides with your passions and interests rather than financial needs.

Setting Clear Goals

Setting clear, measurable goals is vital before embarking on financial independence. Do you wish to be completely free of traditional employment? Are you striving for semi-retirement or the freedom to pursue a passion project without fear of losing your job? Defining your goals will direct your course.

1.2: Why Pursue Financial Independence

Freedom and Autonomy

Financial independence has numerous advantages. One of the most important benefits is the independence it affords. Consider getting up every day with the option of working on tasks that motivate you or spending quality time with loved ones. Financial independence provides you with this freedom.

Security and Peace of Mind

You get peace of mind by ensuring your financial future. You won't have to be concerned about unanticipated financial crises, job loss, or economic downturns interfering with your capacity to sustain yourself and your family.

Fulfilling Your Aspirations

Financial independence allows you to pursue your dreams and aspirations without financial limits. FI makes it feasible to explore the world, start a business, or devote time to charities.

Real-Life Success Stories

We have encountered real-life examples of people who have achieved financial independence by utilizing various passive income sources. These stories motivate and demonstrate people's multiple paths to achieve FI.

1.3: The Role of Passive Income

Passive Income Defined

Passive income is at the heart of financial independence. Passive income is money produced with little or no effort from you. It is revenue created by investments, businesses, or assets that do not require daily engagement.

Contrasting Passive and Active Income

It is critical to understand the distinction between passive and active income. Active income is earned by exchanging your time and effort for money, most commonly through a job. Passive income, however, comes in even when you're not actively working, giving you more time to accomplish what you want.

The Power of Compounding

Passive income sources frequently have the advantage of compounding, which means that your original investments or efforts multiply over time. This compounding effect speeds up your path to financial independence.

1.4: Assessing Your Current Financial Situation

Taking Stock of Your Finances

Examining your financial condition before commencing your journey to financial independence is critical. This includes calculating your net worth, identifying assets and liabilities, and comprehending your current income and expenses.

Determining Your Starting Point

Knowing your financial situation allows you to create realistic goals and track progress. It is the first stage in developing a complete financial independence strategy.

1.5: Creating a Financial Independence Plan

Charting Your Path

A well-defined plan is required to achieve financial freedom. Setting defined, quantifiable goals, establishing a timeframe, and detailing the activities you'll take to attain each milestone are all part of this.

Budgeting and Saving

Budgeting and saving tactics that work are critical components of your plan. Learn how to manage your expenditures, cut unnecessary costs, and direct funds into income-generating investments.

Balancing Short-Term and Long-Term Goals

Financial independence preparation is for more than just the far future. It's all about balancing your short-term financial requirements and your long-term goals. Learn how to use your resources properly.

1.6: Overcoming Psychological Barriers

Addressing Common Barriers

The path to financial freedom is frequently fraught with psychological difficulties. Fear, self-doubt, and uncertainty may all stifle your progress. Recognize these obstacles and devise solutions for overcoming them.

Cultivating a Positive Mindset

A healthy financial outlook can help you. Learn how to reframe negative thoughts, stay motivated, and maintain a resilient attitude in adversity.

Staying Motivated

On the road to financial freedom, consistent motivation is essential. Learn how to stay inspired and focused on your long-term goals.

1.7: The Three Stages of Financial Independence

Breaking Down the Journey

Financial freedom is not a one-size-fits-all goal. It is divided into three main stages:

1. **Financial Security:** Achieving stability and reducing financial stress.

2. **Financial Freedom:** Gaining the ability to pursue your passions and interests.

3. **Financial Abundance:** Reaching a level of wealth that allows for significant contributions and legacy-building.

Customizing Your Path

Each level presents its own set of opportunities and problems. Recognize where you are on the route and adjust your tactics accordingly.

1.8: Mapping Your Unique Path

Embracing Individuality

Recognize that your path to financial independence is distinct. When choosing passive income techniques that correspond with your goals, consider your talents, hobbies, and accessible resources.

The Importance of Lifelong Learning

Adaptability and ongoing learning are required. The financial scene is changing, and staying informed allows you to make more informed decisions.

This comprehensive chapter lays the groundwork for your journey to financial independence. It defines financial freedom, discusses its advantages, and emphasizes the function of passive income. It assists you in reviewing your present financial status, developing a customized plan, and overcoming any psychological barriers. It also presents the concept of the three phases of financial independence and underlines the significance of following your path.

Chapter 2: Understanding Passive Income

2.1: Defining Passive Income

What is Passive Income?

Passive income is money that enters your bank account without any effort on your part. It is capital generated by ventures, enterprises, or assets that don't need constant management. Passive income, as opposed to active income obtained through traditional employment, provides financial freedom by decoupling your income from your labor hours.

Passive vs. Active Income

To completely comprehend passive income, it is necessary to contrast it with active income:

- **Active Income:** This is the money you make from doing direct labor. It is the pay you receive from your employment, consultancy fees, or revenue from actively running a business. It comes to a halt when you stop working.

- **Passive Income:** Even when you are not actively working, passive money continues to flow in. It includes revenues from assets (such as dividends and rental income), online enterprises, intellectual property royalties, and other forms of income that require little continuing labor.

2.2: Sources of Passive Income

PASSIVE INCOME STRATEGIES FOR FINANCIAL INDEPENDENCE

Investment Income

Dividend Stocks

Investing in dividend-paying companies delivers regular dividend payments to owners, providing income and the possibility of capital appreciation. Dividends are normally paid out every three months and can be a dependable source of income.

Index Funds and ETFs

ETFs and index funds provide diversified exposure to numerous asset classes, allowing investors to profit from broad market trends. They frequently pay dividends, making them a good source of passive income.

Real Estate Investments

Real estate may be a very lucrative source of passive income. Rental properties generate monthly rental revenue, whereas real estate investment trusts (REITs) provide dividends from their property portfolios.

Bonds and Fixed Income Investments

Fixed interest payments are made regularly on government and business and high-yield bonds. Bonds may be a crucial component of a well-rounded passive income strategy.

Online Income Streams

Blogging

Creating and monetizing a blog can result in passive income through advertising, affiliate marketing, and sponsored content. A well-established blog can become a reliable source of revenue over time.

YouTube and Video Content

Ad revenue, sponsored videos, merchandise sales, and fan support are all ways for content creators on sites like YouTube to make money. Once uploaded, the material continues to garner viewers and produce revenue.

Podcasting

Sponsorships, advertising, listener donations, and premium content subscriptions allow podcasters to monetize their shows. Episodes are always available to listeners, producing revenue.

Self-Publishing Books and eBooks

Book sales in both print and digital versions can earn authors royalties. Self-publishing provides recurring income for the duration of the book's availability.

E-commerce and Affiliate Marketing

Dropshipping and E-commerce

Using dropshipping or e-commerce strategies to run an online store allows for passive income from product sales. Order fulfillment can be streamlined using automation tools.

Affiliate Marketing

Promoting products or services via affiliate links on a website or social media might increase sales commissions. Successful affiliate marketers create content that continues to draw attention and conversions.

Licensing and Intellectual Property

Licensing Your Creative Work

Artists, musicians, and other creators can license their work for usage in various media and earn royalties for each use. Intellectual property can provide income for years, if not decades.

2.3: The Power of Leverage

Leveraging Time and Resources

The potential of passive income to leverage time and resources is one of its most outstanding features. When you carefully invest or generate income streams, your money, and labor can multiply over time, resulting in exponential growth.

Examples of Leverage

- **Real Estate:** Because of leverage, you can use a mortgage to buy a property that yields rental income significantly more than your initial investment.

- **Online Businesses:** Scaling internet businesses sometimes need extra effort but can result in significant income increases through audience growth and automation.

- **Investment Diversification:** Diversifying your investments across asset classes and businesses can help to decrease risk and boost long-term returns.

2.4: The Importance of Passive Income in Financial Independence

The Role of Passive Income in FI

Passive income is essential for financial freedom. It frees you from the confines of traditional employment, giving you autonomy over your time and finances.

Achieving FI with Passive Income

To obtain financial independence, you must amass enough passive income streams to pay your living expenses. When your passive income exceeds your expenses, you have achieved financial independence.

The Intersection of Active and Passive Income

Many people pursuing financial independence initially rely on their active income to create passive income streams. These streams grow in size over time and gradually replace the need for active revenue.

2.5: Passive Income Realities and Myths

Addressing Common Misconceptions

Passive income is frequently romanticized; however, it is critical to understand the realities and refute common myths:

- **It's Not Completely Hands-Off:** Typically, some level of administration or control is required, particularly during the initial setup.

- **Building Takes Time:** Creating significant passive income streams frequently necessitates an initial investment of time and effort.

- **Risk Exists:** All investments involve some level of risk; therefore, due investigation is essential.

- **Diversification Matters:** It is dangerous to rely entirely on one source of passive income; diversification improves stability.

2.6: Cultivating a Passive Income Mindset

The Mindset of Passive Income

Patience, focus, and a long-term perspective are required to cultivate a passive income attitude. It's about knowing that the rewards can be more lasting and fulfilling than instant revenue.

Embracing Financial Education

Invest in financial education to excel at creating passive income. Learn about various income sources, investing techniques, and wealth-building principles.

The Journey Begins

The first step toward financial independence is to understand passive income. With this understanding, you can investigate the many passive income strategies and create your road to financial freedom.

This chapter gives an in-depth look at passive income, from its definition and sources to its significance in financial independence. It delves into the strength of leverage, the junction between active and passive income, and the need to dispel popular myths. Cultivating a passive income mindset is an essential step toward financial independence. With this understanding, you can investigate the various passive income strategies discussed in the following chapters.

Part I: Investing for Passive Income

Chapter 3: Stock Market Investments

Welcome to the world of stock market investments! This chapter discusses one of the most well-known methods of producing passive income. The stock market provides the opportunity for financial appreciation and regular income through dividends. In this chapter, we'll look at the foundations of stock investing and ideas for creating a passive income stream with equities.

Whether you're a seasoned investor or new to the stock market, this chapter will teach you how to use stocks as a passive income source. From dividend stocks to index funds and value investing methods, you'll discover a variety of approaches that can aid in achieving your financial objectives and independence.

Stock market investments can be critical components of your passive income portfolio, and this chapter will provide you with the knowledge and skills you need to navigate this intriguing and potentially rewarding terrain. Let's look at stock market investments and how they fit into your financial independence quest.

3.1: Dividend Stocks

Dividend stocks are a cornerstone of stock market passive income investing. The companies that issue these stocks frequently distribute dividends to shareholders as a percentage of their profits. Dividends are typically per share and can provide a consistent source of passive income.

How Dividend Stocks Work

You become a shareholder in the company when you buy in dividend stocks. You are entitled to a portion of the company's profits as a shareholder. Companies that pay dividends often do so quarterly. However, some do it annually or semi-annually. The board of directors chooses the dividend amounts, usually expressed as a fixed dollar amount per share or as a percentage of the stock's current price, known as the dividend yield.

Benefits of Dividend Stocks

1. **Steady Income Stream:** Dividend stocks can offer a continuous and predictable income stream, making them appealing to investors looking for consistent cash flow.

2. **Historical Growth:** Many dividend-paying corporations have a long history of growing their payouts. This implies that your passive income might rise over time, aiding the fight against inflation.

3. **Portfolio Stability:** Dividend stocks are frequently issued by well-established, financially secure corporations. Investing in them can help to stabilize your portfolio, especially during market downturns.

4. **Potential for Capital Appreciation:** Besides monthly income, dividend stocks can grow in value over time, potentially providing capital gains when you sell.

Strategies for Investing in Dividend Stocks

1. **Dividend Aristocrats and Dividend Kings:** These are firms that have raised dividends for at least 25 and 50 consecutive years, respectively. Investing in such companies can provide a consistent source of growing passive income.

2. **High Dividend Yield Stocks:** These companies have a higher dividend yield than their share price. While they can provide a considerable income, exercise caution and check that the organization is financially sound.

3. **Dividend ETFs and Funds:** Diversification and expert management are provided by dividend-focused exchange-traded funds (ETFs) and mutual funds. They are an excellent option for passive investors.

4. **Reinvest Dividends:** To boost your passive income development, consider reinvesting your dividend income into the same companies or other investments using dividend reinvestment plans (DRIPs).

Risks and Considerations

While dividend stocks can be an excellent complement to your passive income portfolio, you should be aware of the following risks:

- **Dividend Cuts:** Companies may reduce or abolish dividends during economic downturns or financial difficulties. Conduct extensive research to discover financially sound firms with a consistent dividend payment history.

- **Market Volatility:** Dividend stocks, like all other stocks, are vulnerable to market swings. Be prepared for price volatility in the short term.

- **Diversification:** Avoid overconcentration in a particular industry or sector. To spread risk, diversify your dividend stock holdings.

- **Tax Implications:** Depending on your country's tax regulations, dividend income may have tax implications. To understand the tax implications of your dividend investments, speak with a tax adviser.

Conclusion

Dividend stocks are an appealing alternative for investors seeking consistent cash flow, income growth potential, and portfolio stability. You may leverage the power of dividend-paying firms to develop a consistent stream of passive income on your route to financial independence by understanding how dividend stocks function, adopting proper investment strategies, and minimizing associated risks.

In the following sections, we will look at alternative stock market investment options, giving you a comprehensive grasp of how diverse tactics might help you achieve your passive income goals.

3.2: Index Funds and ETFs

Introduction to Index Funds and ETFs

Because of their simplicity, diversification benefits, and potential for consistent returns, index funds and Exchange-Traded Funds (ETFs) have grown in favor among passive income investors. These investment vehicles make it simple to make stock market investments while lowering the need for active management.

The Basics of Index Funds

Index funds are specific kinds of mutual funds that aim to mirror the performance of a particular stock market index, such as the S&P 500 or the Dow Jones Industrial Average. These funds seek to hold all or a representative sample of the equities they follow in the index. You own a portion of the whole market sector represented by that index if you invest in an index fund.

The Essence of ETFs

Exchange-Traded Funds (ETFs) exhibit similarities to index funds in that they are actively traded on stock exchanges, resembling individual assets. Exchange-traded funds (ETFs) commonly aim to replicate and emulate the performance of a specific underlying index, commodity, or asset class. Exchange-traded funds (ETFs) provide passive investors with the advantage of engaging in intraday trading, allowing for the purchase and sale of these funds at any point throughout the trading day. This feature enhances ETFs' appeal due to its increased flexibility.

Benefits of Index Funds and ETFs

1. **Diversification:** Index funds and ETFs provide broad diversification by holding a portfolio of stocks or other assets. Diversification can disperse risk across different sectors and industries.

2. **Low Costs:** These passive investment vehicles frequently have lower cost ratios than actively managed funds, resulting in cheaper investor fees.

3. **Liquidity:** Exchange-traded funds (ETFs) offer investors the advantage of purchasing and selling them at prevailing market prices during trading sessions, providing them with enhanced flexibility and liquidity.

4. **Transparency:** Index funds and ETFs' underlying assets are publicly disclosed, allowing investors to know exactly what they possess.

5. **Performance Tracking:** Because these funds try to duplicate the performance of a particular index, you can readily assess how your assets are performing in contrast to the broader market.

Strategies for Investing in Index Funds and ETFs

1. **Broad Market Index Funds:** Invest in funds that reflect well-established, well-known indices such as the S&P 500 for broad market exposure.

2. **Sector-Specific ETFs:** If you wish to focus on a specific industry or

sector, ETFs that follow particular sectors, such as technology, healthcare, or energy, are available.

3. **Global and International Funds:** Add international or global ETFs to your portfolio to gain exposure to international markets.

4. **Bond and Fixed Income ETFs:** For a well-balanced portfolio, consider fixed-income ETFs, which provide exposure to bonds and other income-generating securities.

5. **Dividend ETFs:** Some ETFs concentrate on dividend-paying stocks, providing investors with consistent income like dividend stocks.

Risks and Considerations

While index funds and ETFs have many advantages, it is critical to be aware of the following risks:

- **Market Volatility:** Despite their diversification, these funds are nevertheless vulnerable to market volatility. Be prepared for price changes in your assets.

- **Tracking Error:** Due to costs and other factors, there may be minor discrepancies between the fund's performance and the index it monitors.

- **Tax Efficiency:** Consider the potential tax effects of buying and selling ETFs. For further information, speak with a tax professional.

Conclusion

Index funds and ETFs make investing in the stock market easy while generating a passive income stream. They are especially well-suited for investors who want to avoid active management and concentrate on a diversified, long-term investing approach. By selecting the correct funds and managing associated risks, you can reap the benefits of these passive investing vehicles as part of your route to financial independence.

In the following sections, we will look at more stock market investment ideas to help you better comprehend the financial markets' passive income potential.

3.3: Value Investing Strategies

Introduction to Value Investing

Value investing is a well-known investment approach promoted by great investors such as Benjamin Graham and Warren Buffett. It entails carefully picking undervalued companies with long-term growth and income potential. This section delves into the principles, methodology, and advantages of value investing as a passive income approach.

The Principles of Value Investing

Several vital principles underpin value investing:

1. **Intrinsic Value:** Investors determine a stock's intrinsic value, or its true worth, using fundamental criteria such as earnings, assets, and cash flow. The idea is to find stocks that are trading below their real value.

2. **Margin of Safety:** Value investors seek a margin of safety by purchasing businesses at a sizable discount to their actual value. This buffer protects against future losses.

3. **Long-Term Perspective:** Value investors often have a lengthy time horizon, holding companies for years or even decades to allow value to emerge.

Value Investing Strategies

1. **Fundamental Analysis:** This entails doing a thorough review of a company's financial documents, including a statement of comprehensive income, statement of financial position, and cash flow statements, to estimate its financial health and intrinsic worth.

2. **Price-to-Earnings (P/E) Ratio:** Determining a stock's P/E ratio can aid in the identification of undervalued companies. A lower P/E ratio

compared to industry peers may imply value.

3. **Dividend Yield:** Value investors frequently seek out firms with high dividend yields. Companies with a history of dividend payments and sustainable payout ratios are particularly appealing.

4. **Price-to-Book (P/B) Ratio:** Examining a stock's P/B ratio might reveal inexpensive prospects, mainly when it is much lower than the sector norm.

Benefits of Value Investing

1. **Income Generation:** Many value stocks pay dividends, providing a steady stream of passive income.

2. **Risk Mitigation:** Focusing on intrinsic value and a margin of safety can assist in preserving investments during market downturns.

3. **Long-Term Wealth Creation:** As the market acknowledges the stock's true value, value investing can result in significant capital appreciation over time.

4. **Reduced Volatility:** Because value investing focuses on fundamentals, it is less speculative and less vulnerable to short-term market changes.

Risks and Considerations

While value investing has several advantages, it is critical to realize the dangers involved:

- **Timing Risk:** Identifying inexpensive companies may require patience, and the stock market may not always appreciate the value immediately.

- **Company-Specific Risks:** Even undervalued companies can experience issues or inadequate management. Due diligence is required.

- **Diversification:** Rather than concentrating their assets in a few stocks, value investors should maintain a varied portfolio to reduce risk.

Conclusion

Value investing is a tried-and-true approach for generating passive income and building long-term wealth. Investors can uncover cheap possibilities in the stock market by carefully examining underlying value, establishing a margin of safety, and adopting a patient, long-term approach. While value investing has its dangers, a well-balanced approach, extensive research, and diversification can help lessen these risks. Consider value investing an essential component of your passive income portfolio as you work toward financial freedom.

We will continue to investigate numerous stock market investment methods in the following sections, providing you with a comprehensive toolkit to establish passive income streams and work toward your financial goals.

Chapter 4: Real Estate Investments

Real estate investments have long been recognized as a powerful source of passive income. The real estate world offers various chances to grow wealth and secure a consistent stream of passive income through rental properties, Real Estate Investment Trusts (REITs), or novel crowdfunding platforms.

This chapter will look at real estate investments as a strategy for achieving financial independence. We will review the numerous techniques, rewards, and considerations related to real estate investing, providing you with the knowledge and tools to navigate this exciting and possibly rewarding realm.

Real estate investments can be an essential part of your passive income portfolio, and this chapter will help you understand, evaluate, and harness the potential of real estate on your path to financial independence. Let us explore the realm of real estate investments and examine their potential to assist individuals in attaining their financial objectives.

4.1: Rental Properties

Rental properties are a tried-and-true approach for producing passive income from real estate assets. The ownership and leasing of residential or commercial properties have the potential to generate a consistent flow of rental revenue while also potentially capitalizing on the value of the properties in question. This will explore rental properties, addressing fundamental principles, tactics, and considerations for successful passive income creation.

The Basics of Rental Properties

Rental income is the principal source of passive earnings from rental properties. It is the amount tenants pay for the right to occupy and utilize a property. Rental properties exist in various shapes and sizes, including single-family homes, multi-unit apartment buildings, commercial spaces, and holiday rentals.

Benefits of Rental Properties

1. **Consistent Cash Flow:** Rental properties can provide a steady stream of monthly revenue, making them appealing to people looking for dependable passive income.

2. **Capital Appreciation Potential:** Properties may improve in value over time, allowing owners to profit from capital appreciation.

3. **Tax Benefits:** Rental property owners can deduct mortgage interest, property taxes, maintenance expenses, and other expenses, lowering their tax liability.

4. **Protection Against Inflation:** Rental income frequently fluctuates with inflation, assisting in maintaining the purchasing power of your profits over time.

Strategies for Rental Property Investing

1. **Location:** Select properties in desirable areas with high rental demand, decent schools, and easy access to amenities since these qualities can attract quality tenants.

2. **Property Management:** Determine if you will manage the property yourself or engage a property management company to handle tenant relations, upkeep, and other tasks.

3. **Financing Options:** Consider financing options, such as mortgages and financing techniques, to buy rental properties with advantageous terms and low down payments.

4. **Rent Pricing:** Establish competitive and market-driven rental prices to attract and keep tenants while maintaining a healthy cash flow.

5. **Tenant Screening:** Implement a thorough tenant screening process to choose dependable tenants who pay their rent on time and keep the property in good condition.

6. **Maintenance and Repairs:** Regularly maintain and resolve property repairs to satisfy tenants and secure your investment.

Risks and Considerations

While rental properties can provide significant passive income, it is critical to be aware of the following risks and challenges:

- **Tenant Issues:** Dealing with troublesome renters, late payments, or tenant turnover can be disturbing, and competent property management skills may be required.

- **Property Upkeep:** Property upkeep and repairs can be expensive and may necessitate prompt answers to assure tenant happiness.

- • Market Fluctuations: Downturns in real estate markets can affect property values and rental demand.

- **Market Fluctuations:** Real estate markets can experience downturns, affecting property values and rental demand.

- **Regulatory Compliance:** Staying current on local and national laws is crucial for landlords and property managers.

Conclusion

Rental properties are an appealing alternative for generating passive income through real estate investments. You can develop a consistent stream of rental income while benefiting from property appreciation over time by carefully selecting properties, successfully managing renters, and maintaining the property. While there are hurdles and considerations, intelligent decision-making and proactive property management can assist you in capitalizing on the income-generating potential of rental properties as part of your route to financial independence.

We will continue to study numerous real estate investing techniques in the coming sections of this chapter, providing you with a comprehensive toolkit to develop passive income streams and work toward your financial goals.

4.2: Real Estate Investment Trusts (REITs)

Real Estate Investment Trusts (REITs) provide an easy alternative to investing in income-producing real estate assets. REITs are intended to give investors a portion of the income generated by a diverse portfolio of real estate properties. This section will explore REITs' structure, benefits, investing techniques, and considerations for generating passive income through these investment vehicles.

The Basics of REITs

A **Real Estate Investment Trust (REIT)** is a business or trust that owns, operates, or funds income-producing real estate assets. Residential and commercial properties, office buildings, hotels, shopping centers, and other assets may be included. REITs are required by law to pay out at least 90% of their taxable revenue in dividends to shareholders, making them an appealing option for investors seeking consistent income.

Types of REITs

1. **Equity REITs:** These REITs generally own and run income-producing real estate properties. Their principal sources of revenue are rental income and capital appreciation.

2. **Mortgage REITs (mREITs):** Rather than owning actual properties, mREITs invest in mortgage-backed securities and loans. They make money primarily from interest rate spreads.

3. **Hybrid REITs:** Hybrid REITs combine the characteristics of equity and mortgage REITs, allowing them to diversify their revenue sources.

Benefits of Investing in REITs

1. **Passive Income:** REITs are well-known for their periodic dividend distributions, which provide investors with a steady stream of passive income.

2. **Diversification:** REITs frequently possess a diverse portfolio of properties, which reduces the risk of investing in a single property.

3. **Liquidity:** Real Estate Investment Trust (REIT) shares are actively traded on various stock exchanges, providing investors with a high level of liquidity and the ability to acquire or divest shares swiftly.

4. **Professional Management:** Skilled REIT professionals handle property management, tenant relations, and other operational issues.

5. **Accessibility:** REITs enable individuals to participate in real estate without purchasing and managing actual assets.

Strategies for Investing in REITs

1. **Asset Class Selection:** Select REITs that match your investing objectives, whether they are in the residential, commercial, industrial, or specialty real estate sectors.

2. **Diversification:** To spread risk, consider diversifying your REIT assets across different sectors and geographic regions.

3. **Dividend Reinvestment:** Reinvest REIT dividends to acquire additional shares, potentially boosting your passive income.

4. **Regular Monitoring:** Stay current on the performance of your chosen REITs and any changes in their strategy or holdings.

Risks and Considerations

While REITs have various advantages, it is critical to be aware of the following risks and considerations:

- **Sensitivity to Interest Rates:** The sensitivity of real estate investment trusts (REITs) to changes in interest rates can impact their borrowing expenses and prospective revenue.

- **Market Volatility:** REITs, like other stocks, can experience market volatility, so expect short-term swings.

- **Taxation:** REIT dividends may be taxed, so consult a tax adviser to understand the tax consequences of your investments.

- **Management Quality:** Consider the REIT sponsor or management team's track record and management quality before investing.

Conclusion

Real Estate Investment Trusts (REITs) offer a straightforward and easy way to invest in income-producing real estate assets and generate a steady stream of passive income. You may harness the income-generating potential of REITs as part of your route to financial independence by selecting the correct types of REITs, diversifying your portfolio, and remaining informed about their performance.

We will continue to study numerous real estate investing techniques in the coming sections of this chapter, giving you a comprehensive toolkit to develop passive income streams and work toward your financial goals.

4.3: Real Estate Crowdfunding

Real Estate Crowdfunding is a cutting-edge and unique way of real estate investing that allows individuals to participate in real estate projects with minimal contributions. It uses technology and online platforms to connect investors with real estate possibilities, allowing them to access various assets and projects. This will look into Real Estate Crowdfunding, its methods, benefits, and considerations for generating passive income using this approach.

The Basics of Real Estate Crowdfunding

Real Estate Crowdfunding involves several investors pooling their cash to finance real estate projects such as residential developments, commercial assets, or rental properties. Crowdfunding platforms encourage these investments and frequently provide various projects to pick from. Investors can put up as little as a few hundred dollars, making it a viable choice for those with low funds.

Types of Real Estate Crowdfunding

1. **Equity Crowdfunding:** Investors in this model purchase equity or ownership shares in a specific real estate project. They are entitled to a portion of the project's income and possible appreciation.

2. **Debt Crowdfunding:** This involves investors providing loans to real estate developers or creditors as a form of financial support. They receive regular interest payments and the restoration of their principal upon maturity in exchange.

3. **Hybrid Crowdfunding:** This incorporates equity and debt crowdfunding components, allowing investors to invest in ownership shares or fixed-income securities.

Benefits of Real Estate Crowdfunding

1. **Diversification:** Crowdfunding platforms provide access to diverse real estate projects, allowing investors to diversify their portfolios across different property kinds and regions.

2. **Accessibility:** Real Estate Crowdfunding platforms often have modest investment minimums, making them accessible to a broader spectrum of investors.

3. **Passive Income:** Without the requirement for active property maintenance, investors can obtain passive income from rental income distributions or interest payments.

4. **Professional Management:** Crowdfunding platforms frequently collaborate with skilled real estate professionals to manage project management and operations.

5. **Lower Barriers to Entry:** Crowdfunding lowers financial entrance barriers, allowing for involvement in real estate ventures without the need for considerable funds.

Strategies for Real Estate Crowdfunding

1. **Due Diligence:** Conduct extensive research on crowdfunding sites, initiatives, and sponsors. Examine their track records, financial stability, and performance in the past.

2. **Diversification:** Spread your investments across numerous projects to reduce risk and maximize passive income potential.

3. **Risk Assessment:** Understand the hazards involved with each type of investment (equity, debt, and hybrid) and estimate your risk tolerance accordingly.

4. **Monitoring:** Keep track of your assets regularly and stay current on

project developments and financial performance.

Risks and Considerations

While Real Estate Crowdfunding has distinct advantages, it is critical to be aware of the following risks:

- **Lack of Liquidity:** Crowdfunding investments are sometimes illiquid, which means your money may be locked up for the project's life.

- **Regulatory Changes:** Keep an eye on shifting crowdfunding legislation to ensure compliance and the protection of your money.

- **Project Risks:** Market volatility, delays, or unforeseen obstacles might impact real estate projects.

- **Platform Reliability:** Evaluate the platform's dependability and repute to verify it meets necessary security and compliance standards.

Conclusion

Real Estate Crowdfunding offers a simple and novel approach to engaging in real estate investments while creating a passive income stream. You can use the benefits of Real Estate Crowdfunding as part of your route to financial independence by completing due research, diversifying your assets, and carefully monitoring your portfolio.

We will continue to study numerous real estate investing techniques in the following sections, providing you with a comprehensive toolkit to develop passive income streams and work toward your financial goals.

Chapter 5: Bonds and Fixed Income Investments

Bonds and Fixed Income Investments are critical components of a well-diversified passive income strategy. These investments provide a consistent income stream while posing a lesser risk than shares. This chapter will delve into the world of bonds and fixed-income instruments, learning about the numerous types, techniques, and factors to consider while maximizing their income-generating potential.

Bonds and fixed-income investments are diverse and dependable solutions for conservative investors seeking stability or diversifying their passive income sources. This chapter will provide the knowledge and tools you need to comprehend, evaluate, and use the potential of fixed-income assets on your path to financial independence. Let's explore bonds and fixed-income investments and see how they might help you achieve your financial goals.

5.1: Government Bonds

Government bonds, often known as sovereign bonds or treasuries, are among the most secure and well-known fixed-income assets. These bonds, which governments issue at various levels (national, state, or municipal), are considered a cornerstone of fixed-income investing. In this section, we'll dive into government bonds, looking at their characteristics, types, benefits, and strategies for adding them to your passive income portfolio.

The Basics of Government Bonds

The government issues debt instruments called "government bonds" to raise money for various purposes, including financing government operations, infrastructure improvements, and debt refinancing. When you buy a government bond, you effectively lend money to the government, which commits to pay you periodic interest payments (coupon payments) and repay the bond's face value (par value) at maturity.

Types of Government Bonds

1. **Treasury Bonds:** These are bonds issued by national governments, such as the United States Treasury, with longer maturities (10 years or more) and pay set interest semi-annually.

2. **Treasury Notes:** Treasury notes are similar to government bonds but have shorter maturities (usually 2 to 10 years).

3. **Treasury Bills (T-Bills):** Short-term government securities maturing in a few days to a year. T-bills are often sold at a

discount and do not pay interest regularly; investors get the face value at maturity.

4. **Municipal Bonds:** These are issued by state and local governments and serve to finance public infrastructure projects. Municipal bond interest income is frequently free from federal income taxes and, in some situations, state and local taxes.

Advantages of Government Bonds

1. **Safety:** Government bonds are regarded as one of the safest investments because they are backed by the government issuer's full faith and credit.

2. **Steady Income:** Government bonds produce predictable interest payments, providing a steady source of passive income.

3. **Diversification:** They can be used to diversify a low-risk investing portfolio.

4. **Liquidity:** Government bonds are highly liquid and traded in the secondary market.

5. **Capital Preservation:** Fixed-maturity bonds return the face value at maturity, assisting in the preservation of invested money.

Strategies for Government Bond Investing

1. **Ladder Strategy:** Purchase bonds with staggered maturities to build a bond ladder. This technique generates consistent income while mitigating interest rate risk.

2. **Tax Considerations:** Consider tax-advantaged government bonds, such as municipal bonds, for tax-efficient investing.

3. **Reinvestment:** To compound your passive income over time, reinvest coupon payments or matured bonds into new government bonds.

4. **Yield Curve Analysis:** Examine the yield curve to determine interest rate developments and adjust your bond portfolio as needed.

Risks and Considerations

While government bonds are generally low-risk investments, it is critical to be aware of the following potential risk factors:

- **Interest Rate Risk:** Bond values may fluctuate when interest rates change. There is a negative correlation between bond prices and interest rates, such that an increase in interest rates is likely to decrease bond prices.

- **Inflation Risk:** Fixed coupon payments may lose buying power if inflation rates exceed the bond's yield.

- **Credit Risk:** While national government bonds are often regarded as risk-free, investors in municipal bonds should exercise caution because credit risk varies by issuer.

- **Liquidity Risk:** Government bond secondary market liquidity might change, affecting your ability to acquire or sell at desired prices.

Conclusion

Government bonds provide stability in the area of fixed-income investments. They provide a consistent source of passive income while emphasizing capital preservation. You can effectively incorporate government bonds into your passive income portfolio as you work toward financial independence by knowing the many types of government bonds, executing appropriate methods, and being educated about potential hazards.

We will continue to investigate various fixed-income investment methods in the coming sections of this chapter, expanding your awareness of passive income options in the realm of bonds and fixed-income instruments.

5.2: Corporate Bonds

Corporate bonds are a prominent fixed-income because they allow investors to generate regular interest income by lending money to firms. They are well-known for their income-generating potential and are available in various risk profiles. In this section, we'll delve into the world of bonds, looking at their characteristics, benefits, risks, and techniques for incorporating them into your passive income portfolio.

The Basics of Corporate Bonds

Corporate bonds are debt securities corporations issue to solicit funds for issues like expansion, financing operations, or refinancing existing debt. When you buy a corporate bond, you effectively lend money to the issuing business, which pledges to pay you periodic interest payments (coupon payments) and refund the bond's face value (par value) at maturity.

Types of Corporate Bonds

1. **Investment-Grade Bonds:** These bonds are issued by financially secure and creditworthy firms. They are less likely to default and have higher credit ratings.

2. **High-Yield Bonds (Junk Bonds):** Companies with poor credit ratings issue high-yield bonds. They provide higher interest rates to compensate for the greater risk of default.

3. **Convertible Bonds:** Convertible bonds allow bondholders to convert their bonds into a specified number of common stock shares of the company, potentially generating capital appreciation.

4. **Callable Bonds:** Bonds with a call option allow the issuer to redeem them before they mature, which could change the yield and investor returns.

Benefits of Corporate Bonds

1. **Regular Income:** Corporate bonds are a reliable source of passive income since they consistently pay interest.

2. **Diversification:** They can be valuable in diversifying an investing portfolio, especially when combined with other asset groups.

3. **Risk-Adjusted Returns:** Keep an eye on the yield curve and select bonds corresponding to your interest rate assumptions and income objectives.

4. **Maturity Options:** Corporate bonds have different maturities, allowing investors to customize their bond holdings to specific financial goals.

Strategies for Corporate Bond Investing

1. **Credit Analysis:** Conduct extensive research to examine the issuing corporation's creditworthiness, considering credit ratings, financial health, and industry trends.

2. **Diversification:** To limit risk, spread your assets over a range of corporate bonds, including investment-grade and high-yield options.

3. **Yield Curve Positioning:** Monitor the yield curve and select bonds that align with your interest rate expectations and income goals.

4. **Income Laddering:** To limit interest rate risk while maintaining a consistent income stream, build a bond ladder by investing in bonds with staggered maturities.

Risks and Considerations

While corporate bonds have a high earning potential, it is critical to be aware of the following risks and considerations:

- **Credit Risk:** Corporate bonds are susceptible to credit risk, and default is possible if the issuing business experiences financial difficulties.

- **Interest Rate Risk:** Bond values may fluctuate when interest rates change. When interest rates increase, bond prices could decrease.

- **Liquidity Risk:** Some corporate bonds may have reduced secondary market liquidity, limiting your ability to buy or sell at desired prices.

- **Call Risk:** The issuer may redeem callable bonds before maturity, influencing the bond's yield and investor returns.

Conclusion

Corporate bonds are a varied and income-focused solution for investors looking for passive income. You may effectively incorporate corporate bonds into your passive income portfolio by knowing the many types of corporate bonds, undertaking rigorous credit analysis, and applying smart diversification and laddering tactics. While corporate bonds contain credit and interest rate risks, careful selection and ongoing monitoring can help you tap into their income-generating potential as part of your financial independence journey.

We will continue to investigate various fixed-income investment methods in the following sections, expanding your awareness of passive income options in the realm of bonds and fixed-income instruments.

5.3: High-Yield Bonds

High-yield bonds, sometimes called "junk bonds," are a distinctive subcategory of corporate bonds. Companies with lower credit ratings issue these bonds, and their yields are greater to compensate investors for the increased risk of default. In this section, we'll delve into high-yield bonds, looking at their characteristics, benefits, hazards, and strategies for incorporating them into your passive income portfolio.

The Basics of High-Yield Bonds

High-yield bonds are debt securities issued by firms deemed less creditworthy than investment-grade issuers. These issuers may have worse credit ratings because of significant debt levels, questionable financial performance, or industry-specific challenges. High-yield bonds offer higher interest rates, or yields, than investment-grade bonds to attract investors.

Characteristics of High-Yield Bonds

1. **Higher Yields:** Compared to investment-grade bonds, high-yield bonds offer higher-than-average coupon payments, making them enticing to income-focused investors.

2. **Credit Risk:** High-yield bonds have a higher default risk. Therefore, investors should carefully evaluate the issuer's creditworthiness.

3. **Diverse Issuers:** High-yield bonds originate from various industries, including technology, energy, and healthcare.

4. **Maturity Range:** These bonds might have maturities ranging from short-term to long-term.

Benefits of High-Yield Bonds

1. **Attractive Income:** High-yield bonds give investors more interest income, increasing a portfolio's overall yield.

2. **Diversification:** Including high-yield bonds in a fixed-income portfolio can diversify it and provide a source of higher returns.

3. **Capital Appreciation:** If the issuer's financial situation improves, the bond price may rise, resulting in capital appreciation.

4. **Counter-Cyclical:** When issuers' financial problems improve, high-yield bonds may perform well during economic recoveries.

Strategies for High-Yield Bond Investing

1. **Credit Analysis:** Conduct extensive credit research on the issuer to assess its financial health, industry outlook, and creditworthiness.

2. **Diversification:** While high-yield bonds can increase income potential, consider diversifying across issuers and industries to reduce default risk.

3. **Monitoring:** Monitor the financial performance of the high-yield bonds in your portfolio to examine credit conditions.

4. Interest Rate Sensitivity: Be mindful that high-yield bonds might be price and yield-sensitive to changes in interest rates.

Risks and Considerations

Investing in high-yield bonds has certain dangers that investors should be aware of:

- **Credit Risk:** Due to the weaker credit quality of their issuers, high-yield bonds are more vulnerable to default risk.

- **Interest Rate Risk:** The bond prices of these bonds may be liable to change as interest rates change.

- **Liquidity Risk:** High-yield bonds may have less liquidity, which means they may be more challenging to buy or sell in the secondary market.

- **Sector and Industry Risk:** Because some high-yield bonds are focused on specific industries, investors may be exposed to industry-specific risks.

Conclusion

High-yield bonds can help diversify a fixed-income portfolio while increasing income possibilities. Investors can utilize the income-generating potential of high-yield bonds while reducing related risks by doing comprehensive credit analysis, diversifying, and remaining alert. While high-yield bonds have a more significant risk profile, careful selection and monitoring can help you capitalize on the potential returns as part of your route to financial independence.

We will continue to investigate various fixed-income investment methods in the following sections, expanding your awareness of passive income options in the realm of bonds and fixed-income instruments.

Chapter 6: Alternative Investments

While traditional assets such as equities and bonds are the cornerstone of many investment portfolios, alternative investments offer a more exciting and diverse approach to passive income creation. This chapter delves into various alternative investment alternatives, including tangible assets such as real estate and commodities, venture capital, private equity, etc. Alternative investments provide separate revenue streams and can help you achieve financial independence.

In this chapter, we'll look at alternative investments, learning about their distinct qualities, benefits, dangers, and techniques for incorporating them into your passive income portfolio. Whether you want to diversify your income sources or explore new options, this chapter will provide the knowledge and insights you need to navigate the world of alternative investments and achieve your financial objectives. Let's look into alternative investments and see how they might help you on your way to financial independence.

6.1: Peer-to-Peer Lending

P2P lending, often known as marketplace lending, is a rising star in alternative investments. Individuals can function as lenders in this unique strategy, delivering loans to borrowers via Internet channels. The popularity of peer-to-peer (P2P) lending has experienced significant growth due to the opportunity for passive income generated by earning interest on loans while avoiding traditional financial intermediaries. This section delves into peer-to-peer lending, looking at its mechanics, benefits, hazards, and tactics for properly incorporating it into your passive income portfolio.

The Basics of Peer-to-Peer Lending

Peer-to-Peer lending services connect those looking for loans with people ready to fund those loans. The loan process usually goes as follows:

1. **Borrower Application:** Borrowers apply for loans using P2P lending platforms, providing information about their creditworthiness, loan purpose, and preferred terms.

2. **Loan Listings:** Loan listings are prepared based on borrower applications, specifying the loan amount, interest rate, and risk profile.

3. **Investor Selection:** Investors examine available loan listings, choose which loans to sponsor, and commit their funds.

4. **Loan Funding:** After a group of investors has successfully provided complete financing for a loan, the borrower is granted the loan amount, and interest payment commences.

5. **Payment Distribution:** Investors receive a percentage of the borrower's monthly loan payments, which include principal and interest.

Benefits of Peer-to-Peer Lending

1. **Regular Income:** Interest payments from P2P lending can provide a regular source of monthly revenue.

2. **Diversification:** Investors can spread their funds over multiple loans.

3. **Accessibility:** Because P2P lending platforms sometimes have modest minimum investment requirements, they are accessible to a broad spectrum of investors.

4. **Control:** Investors can choose specific loans to customize their portfolios to their risk tolerance and income objectives.

5. **Potentially Higher Returns:** When compared to traditional fixed-income investments, P2P lending can offer competitive interest rates.

Strategies for P2P Lending

1. **Diversification:** Diversify your investments among numerous lenders to spread risk. Avoid putting too much money into a single loan.

2. **Risk Assessment:** To make informed investment selections, thoroughly assess borrower characteristics, credit history, and loan reasons.

3. **Auto-Investing:** Some platforms have auto-investing features, which automatically allocate funds to loans depending on the criteria you provide.

4. **Reinvestment:** To compound your gains, reinvest collected interest

and principal payments into new loans.

Risks and Considerations

While peer-to-peer lending has considerable revenue possibilities, it is vital to possess an understanding of potential hazards:

- **Default Risk:** Borrowers may fail on their loans, causing investors to suffer losses.

- **Liquidity Risk:** P2P loans frequently have fixed maturities, so your capital may be locked up until the loans expire.

- **Platform Risk:** The dependability and reputation of the P2P lending platform you select can impact the safety of your assets.

- **Regulatory Changes:** Stay current on changes in the P2P lending market that may alter the landscape.

Conclusion

For individuals looking for passive income, peer-to-peer lending offers a vibrant and accessible alternative investment opportunity. You may leverage the income-generating potential of P2P lending as part of your route to financial independence by embracing diversification, doing thorough risk assessments, and employing efficient investment techniques. While there are risks associated with default and platform-related concerns, P2P lending provides a unique opportunity to diversify your income sources and work toward your financial goals.

We will continue to investigate several alternative investment techniques in the following sections, expanding your awareness of passive income options outside standard asset classes.

6.2: Crowdfunding Campaigns

Crowdfunding campaigns are a modern technique for investing in startups and small enterprises, allowing individuals to participate in entrepreneurial projects. This alternative investment will enable investors to contribute funds to early-stage firms, real estate developments, or creative ventures in exchange for a potential portion of earnings or other incentives. This section will delve into crowdfunding projects, investigating their mechanics, benefits, hazards, and techniques for incorporating them into your passive income portfolio.

The Basics of Crowdfunding Campaigns

Crowdfunding campaigns entail raising money from a large number of people, usually through online platforms. While crowdfunding is divided into several categories, we will concentrate on investment crowdfunding, which covers equity crowdfunding and real estate crowdfunding.

1. **Equity Crowdfunding:** Investors buy stock (equity) in startups or small firms, becoming shareholders and potentially obtaining a piece of the company's future revenues.

2. **Real Estate Crowdfunding:** Investors contribute funds to real estate projects such as residential or commercial developments in exchange for rental income, property appreciation, or interest payments.

Advantages of Crowdfunding Campaigns

1. **Diversification:** Investing in multiple businesses or real estate developments might help diversify your wealth.

2. **Access to Early-Stage Investments:** Investors can engage in early-stage ventures with high return potential.

3. **Hands-Off Investing:** Compared to direct ownership, crowdfunding often necessitates less active involvement in investment management.

4. **Potential for High Returns:** If the venture or project succeeds, successful crowdsourcing investments can produce considerable profits.

5. **Supporting Innovation:** Crowdfunding allows you to support innovative firms and creative projects in which you believe.

Crowdfunding Campaigns Strategies

1. **Research and Due Diligence:** Before committing funds, thoroughly examine the crowdfunding platform, the project or firm, and the terms of the investment.

2. **Diversification:** Spread your assets across several crowdfunding platforms to reduce risk and maximize possible returns.

3. **Risk Assessment:** Evaluate the risk profile of each investment, taking into account elements such as the business plan, market potential, and project management team expertise.

4. **Regular Monitoring:** Stay current on the status of your crowdfunding investments and company or project developments.

Risks and Considerations

While crowdfunding projects provide excellent prospects, they also pose some risks:

- **Startup Risk:** Many businesses fail, and investors may lose their money if the company fails.

- **Lack of Liquidity:** Crowdfunding investments may have limited liquidity, making it difficult to sell or withdraw capital.

- **Regulatory Compliance:** Because crowdfunding investments are subject to regulatory restrictions that differ by nation, it is vital to comprehend the legal structure that regulates one's investments.

- **Platform Risk:** The dependability and reputation of the crowdfunding platform you select can impact the safety of your assets.

Conclusion

Crowdfunding campaigns enable involvement in entrepreneurial endeavors and real estate developments, providing a new approach to passive income generation. You can utilize crowdfunding campaigns' income-generating potential while helping create new enterprises and creative initiatives by completing research, embracing diversification, and carefully assessing risks. While there are startup and platform risks, crowdfunding is an exciting way to diversify your revenue sources and work toward your financial goals.

We will continue to investigate numerous alternative investment techniques in the following sections, expanding your awareness of passive income potential in the area of alternative investing.

6.3: Cryptocurrency and Blockchain Investments

Cryptocurrency and blockchain investments constitute a novel and quickly evolving area within the alternative investing landscape. These digital assets and decentralized technologies have sparked broad interest due to their potential to create significant returns, although with increased volatility and complexity. This will start on a voyage into cryptocurrency and blockchain assets, covering their mechanics, benefits, hazards, and techniques for incorporating them into your passive income portfolio.

The Basics of Cryptocurrency and Blockchain Investments

Cryptocurrency is a form of digital or virtual currency that relies on cryptographic techniques to secure transactions and control the creation of new units. The system is built upon blockchain, a distributed ledger technology that documents all transactions across a network of computers. The following are essential characteristics of Bitcoin and blockchain investments:

1. **Bitcoin and Altcoins:** Bitcoin (BTC) was the first and most well-known cryptocurrency, but thousands of other cryptocurrencies, known as "altcoins," also exist.

2. **Blockchain Technology:** Blockchain is the foundational technology that underpins cryptocurrencies and exhibits promising potential for utilization across various businesses beyond digital currency.

3. **Exchanges:** Cryptocurrencies are traded on digital exchanges, which allow investors to purchase, sell, and trade these assets.

4. **Wallets:** Cryptocurrency wallets store digital assets and provide secure access.

Benefits of Cryptocurrency and Blockchain Investments

1. **Diversification:** Cryptocurrencies can diversify your portfolio by giving exposure to a non-correlated asset type.

2. **Potential for High Returns:** The cryptocurrency market has seen a significant price rise, providing the opportunity for big gains.

3. **Decentralization:** Blockchain technology encourages decentralization by limiting the power of centralized authorities.

4. **Liquidity:** Cryptocurrencies are traded around the clock, providing investors tremendous liquidity and flexibility.

5. **Innovation:** Blockchain technology fosters innovation in various industries, potentially opening up investment options outside cryptocurrencies.

Strategies for Cryptocurrency and Blockchain Investments

1. **Education:** To make informed decisions, invest time learning the principles of blockchain technology and other cryptocurrencies.

2. **Diversification:** While Bitcoin is the most well-known cryptocurrency, consider spreading your cryptocurrency investments across multiple assets.

3. **Security:** To preserve your digital assets, use trusted cryptocurrency wallets, exchanges, and security measures.

4. **Long-Term Perspective:** Given the cryptocurrency market's volatility, consider investing for the long run rather than speculating in the near term.

Risks and Considerations

Cryptocurrency and blockchain investments carry unique risks:

- **Volatility:** Cryptocurrencies are widely recognized for their inherent price volatility, which has the potential to yield significant gains or losses.

- **Regulatory Uncertainty:** The regulatory framework for cryptocurrencies varies by nation, which might affect investment legality and taxation.

- **Security Risks:** Because cryptocurrencies are vulnerable to hacking, fraud, and theft, security measures are critical.

- **Lack of Consumer Protection:** Compared to traditional financial assets, cryptocurrencies may not provide the same level of consumer protection.

Conclusion

Cryptocurrency and blockchain investments provide a cutting-edge way to diversify your income sources and potentially earn large profits. You may leverage the income-generating potential of cryptocurrency and blockchain assets while navigating the accompanying dangers by educating yourself, applying diversification tactics, emphasizing security, and adopting a long-term view. While they come with volatility and regulatory risks, these investments represent an exciting frontier in alternative investing and can help you achieve financial independence.

We will continue to investigate numerous alternative investment techniques in the following sections, expanding your awareness of passive income potential in the domain of alternative investing.

Part II: Building Passive Income Streams

Chapter 7: Diverse Digital Venture

Part II of this book delves into several digital avenues that provide one-of-a-kind options for creating passive income online. This section looks at various income options, including blogging and video platforms, self-publishing books and eBooks, offering online courses, utilizing affiliate marketing, running e-commerce firms, and licensing creative work.

These digital initiatives allow you to tap into the immense potential of the internet and generate income streams aligned with your hobbies and expertise.

This section's chapters each focus on a specific digital venture, providing deep insights, tactics, and practical success suggestions. Part II will provide the information and tools to efficiently explore these numerous digital prospects, whether you're a fledgling entrepreneur, a content creator, or someone trying to enhance your passive income portfolio. Let's go on a journey of discovery and find out which digital ventures can help you attain financial independence.

7.1: Creating and Monetizing a Blog

Blogging has evolved as a robust technique of making passive income while sharing your knowledge, passions, and insights with a worldwide audience in the digital age. Creating and monetizing a blog allows you to turn your passion into a profit. This section will delve into blogging, learning how to start a blog, develop great material, attract an audience, and efficiently monetize your online platform.

The Fundamentals of Blogging

Blogging entails the regular development and publication of written content on a website. Blogging's key components include:

1. **Choosing a Niche:** Choosing a topic or niche that corresponds to your interests, expertise, and the demands of your target audience.

2. **Setting Up a Blog:** Creating a website or hosting your content on blogging platforms like WordPress, Blogger, or Medium.

3. **Content Creation:** Regularly create valuable, informative, and interesting blog entries on your chosen topic.

4. **Audience Building:** Attracting and retaining readers through effective promotion and engagement.

Strategies for Monetization

You must turn your audience and content into money to monetize your website. The most popular methods of monetization include:

1. **Advertising:** Placing banner ads on your site, such as Google AdSense or affiliate banners, and earning money based on ad clicks or impressions.

2. **Affiliate Marketing:** This entails promoting goods or services using affiliate links to receive commissions for sales from your recommendations.

3. **Sponsored Content:** Collaborating with businesses or companies to create paid sponsored blog pieces or reviews.

4. **Selling Digital Products:** Offering eBooks, online courses, templates, or other digital products related to your blog's niche.

5. **Subscription Models:** Charging readers for premium content or access to exclusive resources through subscription-based models.

Building and Engaging Your Audience

Building and engaging with your audience is essential for successful blogging. Strategies for increasing audience size and participation include:

1. **Consistency:** Publish high-quality content regularly to keep readers returning to your blog.

2. **Social Media Promotion:** To enhance one's online presence, it is advisable to disseminate blog entries through various social media platforms and actively engage with readers within those channels.

3. **Email Marketing:** Creating an email list to engage with your audience directly and advertise new products or content.

4. **Interactivity:** fostering community by encouraging comments, conversations, and feedback.

Time and Effort Required

It's critical to realize that creating a successful blog often requires time and commitment. You might have to work hard to grow an audience and create content before earning money. But with perseverance and smart tactics, your blog can develop into a dependable passive revenue stream.

Conclusion

A dynamic and convenient way to get passive money online is by starting and monetizing a blog. You may turn your blog into a successful business by choosing a topic that aligns with your interests, implementing efficient monetization tactics, and interacting with your audience. Even if success might take time, blogging is fulfilling on your road to financial independence. It offers the possibility of long-term passive income and the chance to share your knowledge and enthusiasm with others.

We will continue to discuss other digital businesses in the sections that follow in this chapter, giving readers a wide variety of chances to think about.

7.2: YouTube and Video Content

Video content is among the most exciting and lucrative internet media types in the digital age. Individuals can make, share, and monetize films on websites like YouTube, making it a potent passive revenue source. We'll delve into the world of YouTube and video content in this section, learning how to launch a channel, make engaging videos, expand your audience, and profitably use video material.

How to Begin on YouTube

1. **Channel Creation:** Create a YouTube channel to start. Pick a channel

name that accurately describes your niche and content.

2. **Content Planning:** Establish your target market and niche. Create a content strategy for your videos with distinct objectives and topics.

3. **Video Production:** To create professional videos, spend money on high-quality tools like cameras, microphones, and video editing software.

Building and Engaging Your Audience

1. **Consistency:** To keep your audience interested and returning for more, consistently upload fresh videos.

2. **SEO Optimization:** Employ SEO strategies to increase the visibility of your video on Google and YouTube.

3. **Engagement:** Engage with your audience to create a sense of community through comments, social media, and live streams.

Monetization Strategies

1. **Ad Revenue:** Enable adverts on your videos to receive a portion of YouTube's advertising revenue.

2. **Channel Memberships:** Give users access to special content, badges, and emojis in exchange for a monthly subscription through channel memberships.

3. **Merchandise Shelf:** Use the merchandising shelf option to advertise and sell your products directly beneath your videos.

4. **Sponsored Content:** Work with brands or businesses to provide sponsored video content in exchange for cash.

5. **Affiliate Marketing:** In your videos, promote goods or services to earn commissions from sales made via your affiliate links.

How to Expand Your YouTube Channel

1. **Collaborations:** Collaborating with other YouTubers can help you reach new viewers for your channel.

2. **Diversification:** To reach a wider audience, broaden your content categories and experiment with various video forms.

3. **Metrics and Analytics:** Analyze your channel's performance frequently using YouTube Analytics to find areas for expansion.

Time and Patience

Creating a popular YouTube channel and earning a passive income often takes time, patience, and determination. Gaining a sizable audience and beginning to generate sizable earnings from your videos may take some time. For your channel to be successful over the long run, consistency, high-quality content, and audience interaction are essential.

Conclusion

YouTube and video content development provide a flexible and highly accessible route to passive income. You may use this platform's earning potential while distributing your original material to the world by creating a channel, making exciting videos, building a following, and experimenting with various monetization tactics. YouTube is an appealing alternative on your path to financial independence, even though it could take some time to develop a successful channel since you have the chance to transform your hobby into a lucrative business.

We will continue to look at numerous Internet businesses in the sections that follow in this chapter. Each offers a unique set of success factors and tactics for diversifying your passive income.

7.3: Podcasting for Passive Income

Podcasting has become a vibrant and significant medium for reaching a global audience with material, stories, and expertise. Furthermore, it provides a unique opportunity to create passive money while doing something you enjoy. This will delve into podcasting, covering topics such as launching a podcast, generating captivating episodes, building an audience, and efficiently monetizing your audio output.

How to Get Started with Podcasting

1. **Create a Concept for Your Podcast:** Define your podcast's theme, niche, and target audience. Choose a topic that piques your curiosity and corresponds to your expertise.

2. **Planning and Structure:** Create a content strategy that includes episode subjects, formats, and a release timetable for each episode. Take into account the duration and frequency of your episodes.

3. **Recording Equipment:** To ensure professional sound quality, invest in high-quality recording equipment such as microphones, headphones, and audio editing software.

Making Interesting Podcast Episodes

1. **Content Creation:** Create episode content that is well-researched and informative. Your episodes should have a clear beginning, core material, and a captivating ending.

2. **Interviews and Guests:** To attract a larger audience, invite relevant professionals, influencers, or guests to share unique insights.

3. **Audio Quality:** Record in a calm environment, use pop filters, and cut out background noise to ensure outstanding audio quality.

Building and Engaging Your Podcast Audience

1. **Consistency:** Publish episodes regularly to keep your audience interested and returning for new information.

2. **Promotion:** Share your podcast on social media, in relevant online communities, and through email newsletters to expand your reach.

3. **Engagement:** Encourage listener engagement by asking for reviews, feedback, and audience questions.

Strategies for Monetization

1. **Advertising and Sponsorships:** Collaborate with businesses or brands to secure sponsorships and adverts for your episodes.

2. **Listener Support:** Accept money or contributions from listeners via platforms like Patreon or Ko-fi.

3. **Affiliate Marketing:** In your episodes, promote items or services and earn commissions on sales via affiliate links.

4. **Premium Content:** Provide paid subscribers with premium or exclusive episodes or content.

5. **Merchandise:** Sell podcast-related stuff, such as branded items or items with quotes or artwork from your program.

Expanding Your Podcast

1. **Collaborations:** Work with other podcasters or industry experts to cross-promote and build your following.

2. **Diversification:** consider diversifying your podcasting portfolio by releasing new shows or spin-offs to cater to different hobbies or niches.

3. **Analytics:** Track listener demographics, engagement data, and episode performance with podcast analytics tools.

Time and Patience

It's crucial to realize that creating a successful podcast and producing substantial passive revenue might take time. As your podcast gains popularity, so will its audience, sponsorships, and cash. Long-term success requires consistency, high-quality content, and audience engagement.

Conclusion

Podcasting is a dynamic and exciting way to generate passive money.

You may turn your passion into a viable venture by beginning your podcast, providing interesting material, encouraging audience participation, and experimenting with various monetization tactics. While the path to financial independence via podcasting may take time, the potential to reach and engage with a worldwide audience while earning money makes it an appealing choice.

In the following sections, we will look at several digital avenues that offer the potential to multiply your passive income online, each with its own set of tactics and success factors.

7.4: Self-Publishing Books and Ebooks

Self-publishing has transformed literature and content creation, allowing content creators and authors to share their content with worldwide audiences independently. Self-publishing books and eBooks help you achieve your creative dreams and provide a potential route for passive income generation. In this chapter, we will look at the art of self-publishing, from writing and formatting to publishing and marketing, to help you make the most of this digital business.

Getting Your Manuscript Ready

1. **Writing and Editing:** Start by creating your manuscript or content. Write, edit, and revise your work meticulously to ensure high quality and readability.

2. **Formatting:** Format your manuscript according to the platform guidelines you plan to publish on, ensuring proper layout, font, and style.

3. **Cover Design:** Invest in a professional cover design that captures the essence of your book and entices potential readers.

Choosing a Publishing Platform

1. **Ebook Publishing:** For self-publishing eBooks, consider sites such as Amazon Kindle Direct Publishing (KDP), Apple iBooks, or Smashwords.

2. **Print-On-Demand (POD):** Explore print-on-demand services like Amazon KDP Print, IngramSpark, or Lulu for physical book publication

3. **Distribution:** Decide whether to publish exclusively on one platform or use multiple platforms to reach a broader audience.

Pricing and Royalties

1. **Pricing Strategy:** Set reasonable rates for your books or eBooks based on genre, length, and market demand.

2. **Royalties:** Understand your selected platform's royalty structures and calculate possible earnings per sale.

Promotion and marketing

1. **Book Description:** Write an engaging book description highlighting your work's primary selling elements.

2. **Author Branding:** Create an author website, blog, and social media presence to establish a strong author brand.

3. **Promotional Strategies:** Utilize strategies like email marketing, book giveaways, and social media advertising to promote your books.

Monetization Strategies

1. **Sales Revenue:** Earn royalties on each book or eBook sold, with the possibility for continued passive income.

2. **Series and Sequels:** Create a book series to attract readers to buy numerous titles.

3. **Audio and Foreign Rights:** Consider selling audiobooks or foreign language translation rights.

Scaling Your Self-Publishing Projects

1. **Write More Books:** Create fresh content regularly to increase your

catalog and acquire a larger market.

2. **Cross-Promotion:** Work with other authors or use cross-promotion to boost your genre awareness.

3. **Reader Engagement:** Use author newsletters, feedback, and forums to connect with your readers.

Time and Patience

While self-publishing books and eBooks can be lucrative, it frequently demands patience and dedication. Developing a dedicated following and generating significant cash may take some time. Long-term success requires consistency in writing, marketing, and connection with your audience.

Conclusion

Self-publishing books and eBooks is a satisfying way to express your talent, share your knowledge, and generate passive cash simultaneously. You may achieve financial independence while fulfilling your writing dreams by carefully structuring your work, selecting the best publication platform, pricing intelligently, and investing in marketing. While the road to success may take time and work, the potential to interact with readers worldwide and create cash from your literary creations is a rewarding and long-term goal.

In the following sections, we will continue to look at several digital avenues that offer the potential to multiply your passive income online, each with its own set of tactics and success factors.

7.5: Online Courses and E-Learning

The digital era has altered how people receive education and learn new skills. Online courses and e-learning platforms have effectively disseminated knowledge and expertise while providing considerable passive income opportunities. In this chapter, we'll look at the world of online courses and e-learning, from course creation and content development to marketing and monetization, to help you make the most of this digital business.

Identifying Your Niche and Expertise

1. **Choose Your Niche:** Choose a specialty or topic in which you have expertise, experience, and a strong desire to educate.

2. **Market Research:** Analyze the demand for courses in your chosen niche and identify your target audience.

3. **Course Objectives:** Define clear learning objectives and outcomes for your course.

Creating High-Quality Course Materials

1. **Content Development:** Divide your course material into logical modules or parts. Produce interesting video lectures, writing materials, quizzes, and assignments.

2. **Interactive Elements:** To increase student involvement, incorporate interactive features such as discussions, forums, or live Q&A sessions.

3. **Quality Production:** Invest in high-quality audio and video recording equipment for professional course production.

Choosing a Platform and Hosting

1. **Select a Hosting Platform:** Select a respected online course hosting platform such as Udemy, Teachable, or Thinkific.

2. **Self-Hosting:** If you want more control over your material and branding, consider self-hosting your course on your website.

3. **Pricing Plan:** Decide if you want to offer your course for free, as a one-time payment, or as a subscription plan.

Marketing and Promotion

1. **Course Description:** Write a captivating course description that emphasizes the course's value and benefits.

2. **Landing Page:** To attract potential students, create an appealing landing page on your website or hosting platform.

3. **Email Marketing:** Create an email list and utilize email marketing to connect with and engage potential students.

Monetization Strategies

1. **Enrollment Fees:** Earn money by charging students to enroll in classes, with the potential for recurring revenue in subscription-based models.

2. **Course Upselling:** Provide additional materials, coaching, or advanced courses to make extra revenue.

3. **Affiliate Programs:** Work with affiliate marketers to advertise your course in exchange for a commission on sales.

4. **Licensing:** License your course content to other educational institutions or platforms for additional income.

Growing Your E-Learning Business

1. **Course Expansion:** Create several courses within your niche to cater to various skill levels and interests.

2. **Student Feedback:** Constantly solicit student input to improve your courses and build your reputation.

3. **Affiliate Partnerships:** Collaborate with influencers or educational websites to broaden the reach of your course.

Time and Patience

Building a successful online course or e-learning business takes time and work, especially when building your reputation and expanding your student base. Consistent content creation, marketing, and student involvement are critical for long-term success.

Conclusion

Online courses and e-learning are exciting and effective methods to share your expertise, empower others, and make passive money. You can achieve financial independence while making a significant difference in education by recognizing your skill, providing high-quality material, effectively marketing your courses, and experimenting with various monetization tactics. While the journey may necessitate commitment and perseverance, a rewarding and long-term endeavor is the opportunity to give outstanding learning experiences to a global audience.

In the following sections, we will continue to look at several digital avenues that offer the potential to multiply your passive income online, each with its own set of tactics and success factors.

7.6: Affiliate Marketing and Product Recommendations

Affiliate marketing is a dynamic and profitable approach to making passive income by advertising products or services you strongly believe in. You can earn commissions on purchases produced through your affiliate links by offering meaningful product recommendations to your audience. This chapter will go into affiliate marketing, from starting and choosing affiliate programs to efficient promotion and monetization tactics.

How to Begin with Affiliate Marketing

1. **Select Your Niche:** Determine the niche or industry where you wish to concentrate your affiliate marketing efforts. Selecting a specialty that corresponds to your hobbies or expertise is critical.

2. **Research Affiliate Programs:** Find affiliate programs that sell

products or services in your selected niche. Look for programs that have trustworthy merchants and fair commission arrangements.

3. **Join Affiliate Networks:** Consider joining affiliate networks such as Amazon Associates, ShareASale, or CJ Affiliate, which offer access to various affiliate programs in one location.

Selecting the Best Products or Services

1. **Quality and Relevance:** Choose products or services that are of high quality and relevant to the needs or interests of your target audience.

2. **Personal Experience:** Promote products or services you have experience with or believe in whenever feasible. Genuine recommendations are more persuasive.

3. **Affiliate Product Research:** Generate informed suggestions and investigate the affiliate items' features, benefits, and user reviews.

Effective Promotion and Content Creation

1. **Create Valuable Content:** Create content for your audience that educates, entertains, or solves problems. Integrate affiliate product suggestions into your content naturally.

2. **Disclosure:** Be open and honest with your audience about your affiliate ties. Clear your use of affiliate links and any potential commissions you may receive.

3. **Use Multiple Channels:** Use various platforms to promote affiliate products, including your blog, website, social media accounts, email newsletters, and YouTube channel.

Strategies for Monetization

1. **Commission Earnings:** Earn commissions on purchases from your unique affiliate links. Commissions may differ depending on the affiliate

program and product.

2. Performance-Based Bonuses: Some affiliate programs reward you with incentives or higher commission rates based on your performance or the sales you generate.

3. Long-Term Earnings: Earn money in the long run as your affiliate content attracts new clients and produces sales.

Legal and Compliance Considerations

1. FTC Disclosure: Comply with Federal Trade Commission (FTC) rules by adding clear and conspicuous disclosures about your affiliate ties in your content.

2. Tax Consequences: Understand the tax consequences of your affiliate profits and consider seeking advice from a tax specialist.

Increasing Your Affiliate Marketing Efforts

1. Diversify Your Promotions: To increase your income streams, promote a range of affiliate items in different categories or businesses.

2. Analyze and Optimize: Analyze the performance of your affiliate promotions regularly and optimize your strategy based on data and outcomes.

3. Build Trust: Focus on establishing trust with your audience by delivering valuable content and honest suggestions frequently.

Time and Patience

A successful affiliate marketing business may require patience and persistence to develop. Although your initial profits may be modest, your passive income potential can grow considerably as you create trust with your audience and expand your promotional activities.

Conclusion

Affiliate marketing and product recommendations provide a dynamic and accessible way to generate passive money. You can make commissions while offering value to your audience by picking the correct items, creating valuable content, and effectively marketing affiliate programs. While success may not come quickly, being able to monetize your recommendations and provide great items or services to your audience is a gratifying and long-term commitment.

In the following sections, we will look at several digital avenues that offer the potential to multiply your passive income online, each with its own set of tactics and success factors.

7.7: Dropshipping and E-commerce

Along with the dropshipping business model, E-commerce offers an enticing potential to make passive income by selling things online. Dropshipping allows businesses to create online storefronts without managing inventory or shipping products. In this chapter, we'll look at dropshipping and e-commerce, from creating an online store to sourcing products and efficiently marketing your e-commerce enterprise.

Setting Up Your Online Store

1. **Choose Your Niche:** Choose a niche or product category that corresponds to your interests, market demand, and profit potential.

2. **Select an E-commerce Platform:** Select an e-commerce platform that meets your requirements, such as Shopify, WooCommerce (for WordPress), or BigCommerce.

3. **Design and Branding:** Create an appealing and user-friendly website design to ensure visitors have a seamless and delightful purchasing experience.

Product and Inventory Sourcing

1. **Dropshipping Suppliers:** Find trustworthy dropshipping suppliers or

manufacturers who offer a diverse range of products in your selected sector.

2. **Product Selection:** Create a collection of products that correspond with your specialty and cater to the demands or preferences of your target audience.

3. **Inventory Management:** As a dropshipper, you will not keep stock. Instead, as customers make purchases, you will order things from vendors.

Product Pricing and Profit Margins

1. **Pricing Strategy:** Get competitive rates for your products while considering product costs, delivery costs, and targeted profit margins.

2. **Free Shipping:** To entice buyers, consider offering free or discounted shipping and including shipping costs in your pricing.

3. **Upselling and Cross-Selling:** Use upselling and cross-selling tactics to boost average order values and profits.

Marketing Your E-commerce Business

1. **Content Marketing:** To attract organic traffic and engage your audience, create valuable material such as blog posts, product guides, or tutorials.

2. **Paid Advertising:** To reach a larger audience and drive sales, use paid advertising channels such as Google Ads, Facebook Ads, or Instagram Ads.

3. **Email Marketing:** Create and manage an email list to nurture leads, make promotional offers, and recover abandoned carts.

Customer Service and Order Processing

1. **Customer Support:** Provide excellent customer support, including timely responses to questions and practical problem resolution.

2. **Order Fulfillment:** Ensure that orders are filled swiftly and accurately by working with dropshipping suppliers.

3. **Returns and Refunds:** Establish explicit policies for returns and refunds to maintain consumer trust and satisfaction.

Strategies for Monetization

1. **Profit Margins:** Profits are generated by the difference in price between what customers pay and the cost of goods and transportation.

2. **Subscription Models:** Consider offering subscription-based products or services to assure ongoing revenue.

3. **Upselling and Cross-Selling:** Increase income by persuading customers to buy related or complementary items.

Increasing the Size of Your E-commerce Business

1. **Grow Product Catalog:** Always add new products and grow your product choices to attract a larger consumer base.

2. **International Expansion:** Investigate international markets and broaden your global e-commerce reach.

3. **Automation:** Use automation solutions to help with order processing, customer care, and marketing.

Time and Patience

Building a successful dropshipping and e-commerce business takes time and effort. Initial profits may be modest, but with consistent marketing efforts, product expansion, and customer relationship management, your e-commerce venture can become a lucrative source of passive income.

Conclusion

Dropshipping and e-commerce provide a flexible and scalable way to generate passive income. You may build a flourishing e-commerce business by choosing the correct niche, obtaining high-quality products, and effectively marketing your online store. While success may necessitate hard work and perseverance, the ability to develop your online business and reach a worldwide audience while earning money makes dropshipping and e-commerce a worthwhile and long-term venture.

In the following sections, we will continue to look at several digital avenues that offer the potential to multiply your passive income online, each with its own set of tactics and success factors.

7.8: Licensing Your Creative Work

Licensing your creative work is a varied and potentially profitable way to generate passive revenue. If you are a photographer, illustrator, musician, or other content creator, licensing allows you to earn money by providing people the right to use your work for specific purposes. This will delve into creative content licensing, covering everything from understanding licensing kinds to locating licensing possibilities and efficiently managing your intellectual property.

Types of Licensing

1. **Royalty-Free:** Royalty-free licensing allows people to utilize your work for a one-time price without paying recurring fees. This is standard practice for stock pictures, music tracks, and graphics.

2. **Rights-Managed:** With rights-managed licensing, you may specify particular terms and restrictions for each usage, such as duration, geographical scope, and exclusivity.

3. **Creative Commons:** Creative Commons licenses provide users with varying amounts of freedom while imposing certain constraints, such as attribution or non-commercial use.

Preparing Your Creative Work

1. **Quality and Originality:** Make sure your work is of excellent quality and unique, increasing its worth and appeal to potential licensees.

2. **Documentation:** Maintain meticulous records of your creative work, including the date it was created, drafts, and any permissions provided.

3. **Legal Advice:** To further understand your rights and alternatives, speak with a legal specialist specializing in intellectual property.

Finding Licensing Opportunities

1. **Stock Agencies:** Submit your work to stock agencies such as Shutterstock, Adobe Stock, or Getty Images, where buyers can license your content.

2. **Art Licensing Agencies:** Art licensing companies can assist artists and illustrators in promoting their work for various things, such as merchandising, home decor, and fashion.

3. **Music Licensing Platforms:** Musicians can license their music to content creators, filmmakers, and advertising using platforms such as Epidemic Sound or Audiojungle.

Increasing the Visibility of Your Licensing Portfolio

1. **Online Portfolio:** Create an online portfolio exhibiting your work and make it accessible to potential licensees.

2. **Social Media:** Use social media to showcase your work, engage with your audience, and connect with possible clients or licensees.

3. **Networking:** Attend industry events, participate in online communities, and network with people and firms in your sector.

Monetization Strategies

1. **Licensing Fees:** Get paid when someone utilizes your work in their endeavors, whether for a website, advertisement, or product.

2. Exclusivity and Premium Pricing: Charge a higher cost for exclusive licenses, which provide buyers exclusive usage of your work for a set period.

3. Renewals and Extensions: Consider providing choices for license renewals or extensions to generate recurring revenue.

Managing Your Licensing Business

1. License Agreements: Create clear and comprehensive license agreements outlining the conditions, usage rights, and payment information.

2. Enforcement: Monitor the use of your licensed work regularly to guarantee compliance with agreed-upon terms and to take action against unlawful use.

3. Portfolio Maintenance: Keep creating and adding fresh work to your portfolio to attract more licensees.

Time and Patience

Building a successful licensing firm can take time, especially when building your reputation and expanding your licensing portfolio. Long-term success requires consistency in producing high-quality work and marketing your business.

Conclusion

Licensing your creative work is a varied and enjoyable way to generate passive money. You can monetize your creative talents and intellectual property by knowing the many licensing types, preparing your work, discovering opportunities, and effectively selling your portfolio. While success may not be instantaneous, the ability to generate money from your creative pursuits while keeping control of your work is a rewarding and long-term goal.

In the following sections, we will continue to look at several digital avenues that offer the potential to multiply your passive income online, each with its own set of tactics and success factors.

Part III: Passive Income through Entrepreneurship

Chapter 8: Diversifying Your Entrepreneurial Ventures for Passive Income

This chapter looks at many entrepreneurial opportunities that can help you diversify your passive income sources. These tactics offer exceptional chances to make money with varied levels of hands-on involvement, whether trying to launch a new business or diversify your current holdings. We'll delve into entrepreneurship and passive income, covering everything from smartphone apps to subscription box enterprises. We'll give you invaluable insights and methods to help you survive in the always-changing digital environment.

8.1: Starting and Scaling a Subscription Box Business

This chapter examines a variety of business alternatives that can be used to diversify your passive income streams. Whether you are attempting to start a new business or diversify your current holdings, these strategies provide outstanding opportunities to generate money with varying degrees of hands-on involvement. We'll delve into entrepreneurship and passive income, discussing anything from mobile apps to subscription box businesses and providing priceless insights and strategies to help you thrive in the always-evolving digital landscape.

Research and Idea Generation

1. **Choose Your Niche:** Choose a theme or niche for your subscription box. It might be associated with interests in food, beauty, lifestyle, hobbies, or any other field.

2. **Market Analysis:** Conduct in-depth market research to identify your target market's preferences, problems, and willingness to use your service.

3. **Unique Selling Proposition (USP):** The USP (unique selling proposition) Create a compelling USP by determining what makes your subscription box different from the competition.

Product Curation and Suppliers

1. **Product Selection:** Compile a list of services or activities that fit your niche and benefit subscribers.

2. **Supplier Relationships:** Form alliances with distributors or producers to acquire products or produce unique items for your subscription boxes.

3. **Quality Control:** Assure that the products' presentation and general quality fulfill subscribers' expectations.

Subscription Model and Pricing

1. **Subscription Tiers:** To accommodate diverse client preferences, provide numerous subscription tiers (such as monthly, quarterly, or annual).

2. **Pricing Strategy:** Set acceptable profit margins and competitive prices that cover your costs.

3. **Add-Ons and Customization:** Consider adding-on products or customization choices to raise the average order value.

Launching Your Subscription Box

1. **Website and E-Commerce:** Create an easy-to-use website where customers can subscribe, manage their accounts, and discover your offering.

2. **Marketing and Promotion:** Develop a pre-launch marketing strategy to increase your subscription box's interest and anticipation.

3. **Fulfillment and Shipping:** Create a logistics plan for product fulfillment and shipment to ensure subscribers receive their orders on time.

Scaling and Maintaining Profitability

1. **Subscriber Retention:** Use tactics to keep current subscribers, like offering top-notch customer service and frequently changing the contents of your box.

2. **Marketing Expansion:** Investigate numerous marketing avenues, such as influencer collaborations, social media advertising, and email marketing, to entice new subscribers.

3. **Feedback and Adaptation:** Respond to subscriber comments and modify your subscription box according to their preferences and shifting market trends.

Time and Patience

It takes time and work to establish a successful subscription box business. It's critical to realize that subscriber growth and profitability cannot occur immediately. Long-term success mainly depends on consistency, attention to client preferences, and innovative curation.

Conclusion

A dynamic and exciting avenue to generating passive income is available by starting and growing a subscription box business. You can develop a subscription box that connects with your audience and produces long-term, sustainable income by carefully choosing your niche, meticulously curating high-quality products, and regularly adjusting to subscriber input. The opportunity to offer members thrilling experiences and products while developing a successful enterprise is a pleasant goal, even though the road to success may require patience and tenacity.

We will examine further entrepreneurial opportunities for passive income generation in the following parts of this chapter, each with its own set of success-related tactics and factors to consider.

8.2: Building and Selling Niche Websites

Designing, developing, and optimizing websites dedicated to particular themes or sectors constitutes the strategy of building and selling niche websites. These websites can potentially develop into priceless assets that can be sold for a profit in addition to generating passive revenue through advertising, affiliate marketing, or product sales. We'll delve into the realm of specialty websites in this section, covering everything from inspiration and creation to building and marketing techniques.

Ideation and Niche Selection

1. **Niche Research:** To begin, look at potential markets, sectors, or subjects with the potential for demand and monetization.

2. **Keyword Analysis:** Use keyword research tools to find relevant terms in your selected niche with high search volumes and little competition.

3. **Monetization Strategy:** Choose your monetization strategy, such as product sales, affiliate marketing, advertising, or a combination.

Creation and Development of Websites

1. **Domain Name:** Pick a catchy and pertinent domain name that accurately describes your niche.

2. **Content Creation:** Create valuable, SEO-friendly material for your target audience.

3. **User Experience (UX):** Create a layout for your website that is simple to use and provides a positive user experience.

Monetization Strategies

1. **Google AdSense:** Use Google AdSense or other ad networks to advertise your website and get money from clicks and impressions.

2. **Affiliate Marketing:** Promote affiliate goods or services associated with your specialized market and profit from sales made via your website.

3. **Product Sales:** If appropriate, design your physical or digital products and sell them on your specialized website.

Traffic Generation and SEO

1. **Search Engine Optimization (SEO):** Optimize your website for search engines to increase organic traffic. This covers content optimization, backlink building, and on-page SEO.

2. **Content Marketing:** Produce helpful and pertinent material to draw and hold visitors.

3. **Social Media Promotion:** Use social media sites to communicate with your audience and market your website.

Scaling and Selling Niche Websites

1. **Portfolio Building:** Develop and maintain specialized websites to diversify your revenue sources.

2. **Website Valuation:** Evaluate the worth of your specialized website based on variables such as traffic, earnings, and expansion possibilities.

3. **Marketplace Listing:** Place an ad on recognized marketplaces like Flippa or Empire Flippers, offering your specialty website for sale.

Time and Patience

Building and selling specialty websites can be lucrative but frequently takes effort and time. It may take some time for new websites to attract visitors and make a sizable profit, so persistence is essential.

Conclusion

Creating and selling specialist websites is a versatile and potentially lucrative passive income method. You may construct digital assets that not only generate continual revenue but can also be sold for a sizable profit by completing in-depth niche research, producing high-quality content, optimizing for SEO, and testing different monetization tactics. While perseverance and flexibility may be necessary for success, using your knowledge to create worthwhile online pages is a gratifying and long-lasting endeavor.

We will continue to look at several business opportunities for passive income generation in the parts that follow in this chapter, each with its own set of success-related tactics and factors.

8.3: Franchise Ownership as a Passive Investment

Franchise ownership offers a unique chance to put money into proven company ideas with the possibility of passive income. By becoming a franchisee, you can access a tested brand, operational support, and a system already set up for success. We'll delve into franchise ownership in this chapter, covering everything from comprehending the franchise model to tactics for achieving success.

Understanding the Franchise Model

1. **Franchise Agreement:** When you buy a franchise, you agree to terms, costs, and obligations in a franchise agreement. This covers both the initial franchise fees and recurring royalties.

2. **Brand and Systems:** Franchising lowers the learning curve for business ownership by providing access to a well-known brand, established business procedures, and support systems.

3. **Training and Support:** To ensure your success as a franchisee, franchisors often offer training, marketing support, and continuous assistance.

Passive Involvement Strategies

1. **Hire and Delegate:** A critical tactic for passive franchise ownership is to employ qualified managers and personnel to oversee daily operations.

2. **Multi-Unit Ownership:** To boost your potential for passive income while maintaining a generally hands-off role, consider owning many franchise units.

3. **Semi-Absentee Ownership:** Some franchise models are set up for semi-absentee ownership, enabling you to continue running your company or employment while working part-time on the franchise.

Analyzing Potential Franchises

1. **Research and Due Diligence:** Conduct thorough research on franchise options, considering financials, market demand, rivalry, and the franchisor's standing.

2. **Legal and Financial Consultation:** Consult with legal and financial experts with franchising experience to study the agreements and evaluate the potential for opportunities.

3. **Franchise Disclosure Document (FDD):** Review the franchise disclosure document (FDD), which the franchisor has issued and contains essential information regarding the franchise.

Creating Passive Income

1. **Royalty Payments:** As a franchisee, you usually pay recurring royalties to the franchisor. A percentage of these fees goes toward the franchisor's passive income.

2. **Profit Sharing:** Depending on how well the franchise performs, some franchise agreements include profit-sharing clauses that offer passive income.

3. **Resale Value:** A successful franchise unit can provide sizable monetary profits upon sales.

Risks and Considerations

1. **Initial Investment:** Depending on the brand and industry, franchise ownership frequently demands a sizable up-front investment.

2. **Market and Competition:** Examine the market circumstances and rivalry in the region where you intend to set up your franchise unit.

3. **Franchisor Relationship:** To ensure continued support and success, keep a positive and cooperative relationship with the franchisor.

Time and Patience

Even when a franchise operates passively, maintenance is necessary, particularly during the setup and transition phases. However, you may gradually lessen your involvement and benefit from a more passive income stream with efficient delegation and administration.

Conclusion

Franchise ownership as a passive investment provides a way to generate passive income while gaining access to well-known brands and infrastructure. You can succeed as a franchisee and earn money without the demands of ongoing management by comprehending the franchise model, assessing opportunities, and using passive involvement tactics. Although initial investments and due research are necessary, franchise ownership is a desirable alternative due to the possibility of long-term passive income and company growth.

We will continue to look at several business opportunities for passive income generation in the parts that follow in this chapter, each with its own set of success-related tactics and factors.

8.4: Automating an Online Business

A practical method for converting an online business into a passive income source is automation. Utilizing technology and systems will enable you to automate repetitive chores, optimize corporate processes, and build a company that requires little day-to-day management. This section will discuss the art of automating an internet business, covering everything from reaping the rewards to implementing automation techniques.

Benefits of Automation

1. **Time Freedom:** Automation gives you more time to focus on strategic

choices, chances for growth, or even the investigation of new business ventures.

2. **Consistency:** Automated systems consistently complete tasks, lowering the possibility of human error and guaranteeing a high level of quality.

3. **Scalability:** As your online business expands, automation helps you scale it more efficiently without increasing your workload proportionately.

Identifying Opportunities for Automation

1. **Workflow Analysis:** Examine your company processes to find areas that can be automated, such as repeated operations and bottlenecks.

2. **Technology Assessment:** Look into platforms, apps, and software solutions that can help automate particular procedures or tasks.

3. **Customer Interactions:** Look for ways to automate email marketing, customer service, and other contacts while keeping a personalized touch.

Implementing Automation Strategies

1. **Email Marketing Automation:** Employ email marketing tools to segment subscribers, automate email campaigns, and distribute personalized content.

2. **E-commerce Automation:** Automate e-commerce using ordering processing, inventory control, and customer relationship management (CRM) technologies.

3. **Social Media Scheduling:** Use tools for social media management to plan posts, monitor engagement, and assess results.

Outsourcing and Delegating

1. **Virtual Assistants:** If you need help with administrative work,

customer service, or content development, consider employing virtual assistants.

2. **Freelancers and Contractors:** Hire freelancers or contractors with the necessary knowledge for particular projects or functions.

3. **Third-Party Services:** Look into your alternatives for outsourcing tasks like customer service, shipping, and order fulfillment.

Monitoring and Optimization

1. **Data Analytics:** Use data analytics to improve your automation tactics by continuously monitoring key performance indicators (KPIs).

2. **Feedback Loops:** Gather user, employee, or customer input to pinpoint areas where automation might be enhanced or modified.

3. **Security and Compliance:** Ensure automated procedures follow security and legal compliance requirements.

Time and Patience

An online company's automation is a continuous process that may require some time to adapt and optimize fully. Be prepared to invest time in the initial setup of automation and ongoing system reviews and adjustments.

Conclusion

An innovative method of generating passive revenue is through the automation of an online business. You may build a business that runs smoothly, requires little hands-on management, and gives you the advantages of time freedom and scalability by embracing automation options. Although the initial setup and adjustment phases may need work, an automated internet business is well worth the investment in the long run.

We will continue to look at several business opportunities for passive income generation in the parts that follow in this chapter, each with its own set of success-related tactics and factors.

8.5: Passive Income through Mobile Apps

Because of the widespread usage of smartphones, a vibrant ecosystem for mobile app creation has emerged, offering business owners the chance to make passive revenue from cutting-edge, user-friendly programs. This chapter will delve into passive income through mobile apps, covering everything from conceptualization and development to commercialization and long-term success tactics.

Conceptualization and Market Research

1. **Idea Generation:** Generate app concepts that address a particular need, issue, or interest. For validation, take into account doing surveys or requesting user input.

2. **Market Analysis:** Examine the market for mobile apps to spot trends, rivalry, and any openings where your app might stand out.

3. **Target Audience:** Identify your target audience and gain an understanding of their preferences, problems, and behaviors.

Design and Development of Apps

1. **Platform Selection:** Choose between developing your app for iOS, Android, or both platforms. If you need to hire developers, think about leveraging app development frameworks.

2. **User-Centric Design:** Prioritize a logical, user-friendly design that improves user experience and promotes engagement.

3. **Prototyping and Testing:** To receive input, make necessary adjustments, create prototypes, and conduct user testing.

Monetization Strategies

1. **In-App Advertising:** Include adverts in your app using in-house ad

placements or ad networks like AdMob.

2. In-App Purchases: Provide in-app purchases for virtual goods, deluxe features, or content.

3. Subscription Models: Implement subscription strategies to offer recurring access to premium services or content.

App Marketing and Promotion

1. App Store Optimization (ASO): Use relevant keywords, eye-catching graphics, and captivating descriptions to increase your app's exposure in app stores.

2. Social Media Marketing: Use social media sites to promote your app, interact with users, and foster community.

3. User Acquisition: To attract new users, use organic growth techniques, influencer marketing, and digital advertising.

User Engagement and Retention

1. Push Notifications: Re-engage users, deliver updates, and promote app usage using push notifications.

2. Feedback Channels: Create feedback channels within the app to gather user recommendations and address any issues.

3. Regular Updates: Release updates that fix issues, add functionality, and improve user experience to keep your program current.

Tracking and Analytics

1. Data Collection: Use analytics tools to monitor user activity, engagement, and app monetization.

2. A/B Testing: Run A/B tests to improve your apps' functions, designs, and monetization methods.

3. **Revenue Monitoring:** Keep tabs on the revenue sources for your app and modify your strategy in light of performance information.

Time and Patience

Developing a passive income stream using mobile apps can take time, especially in the cutthroat app industry. Having a long-term perspective and being ready to tweak and advance your app continuously is critical.

Conclusion

Building a mobile app that makes passive revenue is an entrepreneurial endeavor that is constantly changing and evolving. You may unlock the tremendous potential of the mobile app industry by choosing a niche, creating user-friendly software, and putting good monetization and marketing tactics in place. While perseverance and adaptability may be necessary for success, providing users with value while generating passive money is a fulfilling and long-term goal.

8.6: Realizing Passive Income from Inventions and Patents

By safeguarding your intellectual property and enabling you to profit from using your protected concepts, goods, or processes, inventions and patents present a distinctive way to generate passive income. We will examine the realm of ideas and patents in this chapter, from conceptualization and patent application to methods for generating passive revenue via licensing and royalties.

Conceptualization and Invention Development

1. **Idea Generation:** Start by generating original concepts for products, services, or solutions that solve specific issues or meet particular demands.

2. **Market Research:** Conduct in-depth market research to confirm your invention's need and determine prospective competitors.

3. **Prototype Development:** To show the viability and functionality of

your innovation, develop a working prototype or proof of concept.

Protection of Intellectual Property

1. **Patent Types:** Understanding the many sorts of patents, such as plant patents for novel plant varieties, design patents for decorative patterns, and utility patents for ideas and methods.

2. **Patent Search:** Conduct a thorough patent search to ensure your innovation is original and hasn't already been patented.

3. **Patent Filing:** Engage the services of a patent attorney or agent's services to aid in preparing and submitting a patent application to the relevant intellectual property office, such as the United States Patent and Trademark Office.

Licensing and Royalties

1. **License Agreements:** After your patent is approved, you can make licensing arrangements with companies or people who want to use the patented technique or item.

2. **Royalty Structure:** Discuss the parameters of the license agreement, such as the exclusivity clauses, royalty rates, and payment schedules.

3. **Monitoring and Enforcement:** To maintain compliance and collect royalties, monitor how your patented technology is used and enforce your patent rights.

Management of Patent Portfolio

1. **Diversification:** Consider assembling a patent portfolio to improve your potential for passive revenue by safeguarding several inventions.

2. **Maintenance:** To maintain your patents in effect and prevent expiration, be aware of maintenance payments and deadlines.

3. **Continual Innovation:** To remain competitive and relevant in your sector, develop new ideas and file patents.

Realization of Passive Income

1. **Royalty Payments:** Royalty payments received from licensees are a form of passive income and are frequently made weekly or annually.

2. **Scaling Opportunities:** The potential for passive income scales with expanding your patent portfolio, providing various revenue streams.

3. **Exit Strategies:** Consider selling your patented technology or negotiating buyout deals with potential buyers.

Time and Patience

It takes time and perseverance to generate passive revenue from patents and ideas. Although the patent application, grant, and licensing processes might be lengthy, the benefits can be significant.

Conclusion

A dynamic and profitable entrepreneurial endeavor utilizes inventions and patents to provide passive revenue. You can develop a dependable passive revenue stream while offering ground-breaking solutions to your business by safeguarding your intellectual property, entering into licensing agreements, and successfully maintaining your patent portfolio. While obtaining a patent may require patience and perseverance, getting royalties for your intellectual works is a worthwhile and long-term goal.

Part IV: Managing and Growing Your Passive Income

Chapter 9: Passive Income Growth Techniques

The many approaches and factors for managing and expanding your passive income portfolio will be covered in this chapter. These include tax planning, asset safeguarding, estate planning, portfolio scalability, risk management, diversification, and retirement planning. In your quest for financial independence, each of these subjects is essential.

9.1: Passive Income Tax Strategies

A key component of maximizing your passive income is tax management. The appropriate tax planning techniques can reduce your tax burden, save more income, and boost your investment's overall return. This chapter will examine various tax planning techniques designed especially for passive income streams.

Investment Accounts That Are Tax-Efficient

1. **Individual Retirement Accounts (IRAs):** Learn about the advantages of Roth and standard IRAs for retirement savings, each with specific tax advantages.

2. **401(k) Plans:** If your employer gives access to a 401(k), consider contributing to minimize your taxable income and improve your retirement savings.

3. **Health Savings Accounts (HSAs):** HSAs can be a valuable addition to your financial portfolio because they provide tax deductions for certain medical expenses.

Taxation on Capital Gains and Dividends

1. **Long-Term vs. Short-Term Capital Gains:** To be eligible for lower

capital gains tax rates, you must understand the tax ramifications of keeping investments for long periods.

2. **Qualified Dividends:** Discover how specific stock dividends may be eligible for lower tax rates, making them a tax-efficient source of passive income.

Tax-Advantaged Investments

1. **Municipal Bonds:** Consider purchasing municipal bonds, which frequently provide federal and sporadically state tax-free interest income.

2. **Real Estate Investment Trusts (REITs):** Research the potential tax benefits of investing in REITs, which can generate regular income.

Rules for Passive Loss

1. **Passive Activity Loss Rules:** Be aware of IRS regulations governing passive gains and losses, as they may affect the ability to deduct losses from passive income.

2. **Real Estate Professional Status:** Discover how to become a real estate professional and how you can deduct expenses related to real estate to offset your rental revenue.

Structures of Entities for Business Income

1. **Limited Liability Companies (LLCs):** Learn about limited liability companies (LLCs), which provide flexibility in the tax treatment of business profits and liability protection.

2. **S Corporations:** Recognize how S Corporations can reduce self-employment taxes and pass-through income tax benefits.

Considerations for International Taxes

1. **Foreign Investments:** When generating passive income from abroad investments or assets, be aware of the tax ramifications.

2. **Foreign Account Reporting:** To avoid fines, adhere to the tax reporting rules for foreign bank accounts.

Consultation and Planning

1. **Tax Professionals:** To create and implement tax-efficient methods customized to your financial circumstances, consider working with tax specialists like CPAs or tax consultants.

2. **Regular Review:** As tax rules and your financial situation change, continuously review and modify your tax tactics.

Conclusion

To maximize your financial advantages while abiding by tax laws, effectively managing your tax plans for passive income is crucial. You may maximize your potential for passive income by investigating tax-efficient investment accounts, learning about capital gains and dividend taxation, and utilizing tax-advantaged investments. A more tax-effective and successful trip with passive income will also result from remaining knowledgeable on passive loss rules, selecting the best corporate structures for business income, and considering foreign tax considerations.

We will continue to discuss additional essential tactics and factors for managing and expanding your passive income portfolio in the following sections.

9.2: Asset Protection and Estate Planning

Managing and increasing your passive income requires careful planning to transfer your estate and efficiently protect your wealth and assets. In this chapter, we'll go into asset protection and estate planning tactics explicitly designed for people who make passive income.

Asset Protection Strategies

1. **Asset Segregation:** Consider organizing your assets to divide them

between personal and business holdings. This can protect personal assets from obligations arising from your business.

2. **Limited Liability Entities:** Consider using corporations or limited liability companies (LLCs) to reduce personal liability for debts or legal concerns arising from your firm.

3. **Insurance Coverage:** To guard against unanticipated incidents or litigation, ensure you have enough insurance coverage, especially liability insurance.

Trusts and Estate Planning

1. **Revocable Living Trust:** To speed up the distribution of assets to beneficiaries and skip the probate procedure, establish a revocable living trust.

2. **Irrevocable Trusts:** For specialized asset protection and estate planning goals, consider irrevocable trusts, such as irrevocable life insurance trusts (ILITs).

3. **Durable Power of Attorney:** Designate a dependable person with a durable power of attorney as your agent to handle financial matters in the event of incapacitation.

Planning Your Estate Tax-Efficiently

1. **Estate Tax Planning:** Understanding estate tax exemptions and thresholds will help you plan strategically to save estate taxes.

2. **Gift Tax Strategies:** Research gifting methods to minimize your taxable estate and transfer assets tax-efficiently to heirs.

3. **Qualified Personal Residence Trust (QPRT):** Consider using a QPRT to give your heirs the title to your primary house while retaining the ability to live there for a set amount of time.

Planning for Business Succession

1. **Buy-Sell Agreements:** Create buy-sell agreements for your company to ensure a seamless transfer of ownership in the case of a partner's passing or retirement.

2. **Key Person Insurance:** Invest in critical person insurance to safeguard your company's financial stability if a crucial person, such as the company's founder, is rendered incapable of working or passes away.

Continual Review and Update

1. **Regular Review:** To ensure your asset protection and estate planning methods align with your evolving financial circumstances and goals, periodically evaluate and adjust them.

2. **Legal Counsel:** To ensure your methods are current and compelling, speak with estate planning lawyers and financial experts.

Conclusion

Managing passive income and securing a secure financial future for you and your heirs requires estate planning and asset protection. You may protect your assets, reduce your tax obligations, and establish a clear plan for transferring wealth by implementing asset segregation, trust establishment, tax-efficient estate planning, and business succession planning. Your road toward passive income will be successful in the long run if you regularly analyze and revise your techniques to keep up with changing conditions and legal requirements.

We will continue to discuss additional important tactics and factors for managing and expanding your portfolio of passive income in the following sections.

9.3: Diversification and Risk Management

The construction and preservation of your portfolio for passive income requires the application of both diversification and risk management strategies. You may safeguard your wealth and improve your ability to manage risk by diversifying your investments across several asset classes. This section will examine risk management and diversification strategies and tactics in the context of passive income.

The Importance of Diversification

1. **Asset Classes:** Diversify your investments among several asset classes, such as equities, bonds, real estate, and alternative investments, to reduce your exposure to any asset class.

2. **Geographic Diversification:** To reduce risks related to local economic situations, consider investing in domestic and foreign markets.

3. **Sector Diversification:** To lower sector-specific risks, diversify within each asset class by investing in several industries (such as technology, healthcare, and finance).

Risk Management Strategies

1. **Risk Tolerance Assessment:** Assess your investment horizon and risk tolerance to ensure your portfolio aligns with your financial objectives and comfort zone.

2. **Asset Allocation:** Based on your risk appetite, time horizon, and financial goals, develop a suitable asset allocation strategy.

3. **Portfolio Rebalancing:** To maintain your target asset allocation and efficiently manage risk, periodically evaluate and rebalance your portfolio.

Passive Income Investments

1. **Income-Generating Assets:** To maintain a consistent flow of passive income, invest in income-generating assets, including dividend stocks, bonds, and real estate investment trusts (REITs).

2. **Diversified Dividend Portfolio:** To spread the sources of dividend income, build a varied dividend portfolio with equities from different businesses and sectors.

3. Alternative Investments: Consider other investments like peer-to-peer lending or crowdfunding to diversify your passive income sources.

Risk Mitigation

1. Insurance Coverage: To minimize unforeseen financial setbacks, ensure adequate insurance coverage, such as life, health, and disability insurance.

2. Emergency Fund: Keep a liquid emergency fund on hand to meet unforeseen costs and avoid using your investments for passive income in times of need.

3. Professional Guidance: To make well-informed decisions and manage risk, seek guidance from financial planners or investing experts.

Passive Income Resilience

1. Multiple Income Streams: To increase financial security and lessen dependency on a single source of income, establish many passive income streams.

2. Conservative Projections: To account for probable market changes and economic uncertainty, utilize conservative predictions when determining your goals for passive income.

3. Continuous Monitoring: Keep an eye on the performance of your investments for passive income and make necessary adjustments to your plans to consider shifting market conditions.

Conclusion

A practical and resilient passive income strategy is built on diversification and risk management pillars. You may reduce risks and safeguard your capital over time by diversifying among different asset classes, using efficient risk management techniques, and keeping an eye on passive income investments. Your risk tolerance, asset allocation, and overall portfolio strategy must be regularly reviewed to ensure they correspond with your financial goals and shifting market conditions.

9.4: Passive Income for Retirement Planning

Many people list their primary financial goal as preparing for a secure and fulfilling retirement. Passive income is essential in assisting you in achieving your goal since it provides a consistent income stream during your retirement years. This chapter will examine the processes and variables involved in using passive income for retirement planning.

Goal-setting for Retirement

1. **Retirement Lifestyle:** Describe your ideal retirement lifestyle, considering travel, hobbies, and housing possibilities, to determine the amount of retirement income you'll need.

2. **Retirement Age:** Choose a retirement age because it will influence your objectives for passive income and retirement savings.

3. **Income Gap Analysis:** Find the difference between your anticipated pension and Social Security income and your planned retirement costs.

Streams of Passive Income

1. **Diverse Income Sources:** To create passive income, combine a diverse portfolio of investments, including dividend stocks, real estate, bonds, and other assets.

2. **Real Estate Investments:** Research real estate investment properties or real estate investment trusts (REITs) for rental income during retirement.

3. **Annuities:** Consider annuities, which provide retirement stability and peace of mind by ensuring income for life.

Tax-Efficient Strategies

1. **Tax-Advantaged Accounts:** Increase contributions to tax-advantaged retirement accounts like IRAs and 401(k)s to reduce taxable income in

retirement.

2. **Roth Conversions:** To potentially reduce your future tax responsibilities on retirement income, consider converting your IRA to a Roth account.

3. **Qualified Dividends:** These dividends may be taxed favorably in retirement; therefore, invest in stocks that offer them.

Passive Income Growth

1. **Regular Monitoring:** Check your portfolio of passive income investments to ensure that it fits your retirement goals and changes in line with the market.

2. **Reinvestment:** Consider reinvesting some of your passive income to increase your portfolio and preserve your purchasing power in retirement.

3. **Lifestyle Adjustments:** Depending on your passive income levels and investment success, you might need to change your retirement lifestyle.

Passive Income as a Retirement Bridge

1. **Early Retirement:** Use passive income to bridge the gap between early retirement and the age at which you can withdraw funds without suffering penalties from conventional retirement plans.

2. **Part-Time Work:** Consider part-time employment or consultancy opportunities to supplement passive income during retirement.

3. **Healthcare Planning:** Prepare for upcoming medical expenses, such as Medicare enrollment and potential long-term care needs.

Conclusion

Passive income is crucial for maintaining financial stability and enjoying a comfortable retirement. By setting clear retirement goals, diversifying your passive income sources, and utilizing tax-efficient strategies, you may build a reliable source of income to sustain your retirement lifestyle. With regular monitoring and adjustments, careful planning, and early retirement, you can achieve financial independence and peace of mind in your retirement years.

The following sections will discuss other crucial strategies and elements for managing and growing your passive income portfolio.

9.5: Scaling Your Passive Income Portfolios

Scaling your passive income portfolio involves purposefully growing your investments and income streams to steadily increase your wealth and financial security. This section will look at ways to improve your passive income for long-term financial progress.

Assessing Your Current Portfolio

1. **Portfolio Review:** Assess the performance and income-generating potential of your current passive income investments by thoroughly analyzing them.

2. **Income Analysis:** Look over your current passive income sources, such as dividends, rental income, interest, and any other sources, to build a baseline.

3. **Risk Assessment:** Assess the level of risk associated with each investment in your portfolio and identify any areas that could be strengthened.

Diversification and Expansion

1. **Asset Classes:** Add asset classes, such as real estate, shares, bonds, or alternative assets, to diversify your portfolio and spread your risk.

2. **Geographic Expansion:** Investigate opportunities to invest in additional markets or regions, both domestically and internationally.

3. **Sector Diversification:** Invest in various sectors or industries within

each asset class to reduce sector-specific risks.

Income-Boosting Techniques

1. **Dividend Growth Stocks:** Focus your investments on dividend-paying companies with a track record of consistent dividend increases to progressively enhance your passive income.

2. **Real Estate Portfolio Expansion:** To increase rental revenue, consider adding new rental properties to your portfolio or considering crowdfunding portals for real estate investments.

3. **Fixed Income Strategies:** To diversify your income sources, consider fixed-income investments like corporate, municipal, or high-yield bonds.

Passive Income Automation

1. **Automated Investments:** Regularly add to your passive income portfolio using automatic investing strategies that benefit from dollar-cost averaging.

2. **Dividend Reinvestment Plans (DRIPs):** Enroll in a DRIP to have dividend income automatically reinvested, boosting your returns.

3. **Robo-Advisors:** Consider using Robo-advisors for automated portfolio management and rebalancing to maximize your asset allocation.

Utilizing Tools and Technology

1. **Passive Income Apps:** Track and manage your costs, passive income sources, and portfolio performance with the help of financial tools and apps for passive income.

2. **Online Research:** Use online tools and research platforms to discover new investment ideas and stay current on market trends.

3. **Financial Advisors:** Talk to financial advisors or investment specialists who can give you advice on the best strategies to scale your portfolio.

Goal Setting and Monitoring

1. **Clearly defined Objectives:** Set timelines for expanding your portfolio and precise passive income objectives, ensuring they align with your long-term financial goals.

2. **Regular Evaluation:** Monitor your portfolio's performance, assess your progress toward your goals, and make appropriate adjustments.

3. **Adjusting Risk Levels:** Consider modifying risk levels as your portfolio expands to maintain a healthy balance between growth and stability.

Conclusion

Scaling your passive income portfolio is a dynamic and ongoing process that requires careful planning, diversification, and a commitment to long-term financial growth. You can progressively increase your passive income by analyzing your current portfolio, diversifying your holdings, implementing income-boosting strategies, and utilizing technology and tools. Setting specific objectives, monitoring your progress frequently, and adjusting your risk tolerance as appropriate will help you become more financially independent.

The following sections will review crucial strategies and elements for managing and growing your passive income portfolio.

9.6: Troubleshooting Common Passive Income Challenges

While passive income has numerous advantageous financial impacts, there are particular challenges. This section will discuss some common barriers that those who generate passive income may encounter and look at solutions.

Challenge 1: Insufficient Income

1. **Determine the Root Cause:** Consider why passive income isn't

generated, such as underutilized assets or low-yielding investments.

2. **Portfolio Review:** Look for underperforming assets in your investment holdings and consider measures to increase income.

3. **Income Diversification:** Consider expanding or increasing your current investments to diversify your income sources.

Challenge 2: Market Volatility

1. **Risk Management:** Reevaluate your risk tolerance and adjust your asset portfolio to mitigate the consequences of market volatility.

2. **Emergency Fund:** Don't rely on your investments for passive income during market downturns; keep a cash reserve to cover expenses.

3. **Long-Term Perspective:** Focus on long-term financial goals and avoid acting hastily in response to fleeting market fluctuations.

Challenge 3: Tax Complexity

1. **Tax Planning:** Use tax-efficient strategies, like increasing contributions to tax-advantaged accounts and reducing capital gains and dividend taxes.

2. **Professional Assistance:** Consult with tax experts or financial consultants who are knowledgeable about the taxation of passive income.

3. **Compliance:** Ensure you're up to date on changes to the tax code and abide by the rules on tax reporting.

Challenge 4: Liquidity Problems

1. **Emergency Fund:** Keep an emergency fund separate from your assets so you can pay bills in an emergency without jeopardizing your passive income.

2. **Regular Cash Flow:** Consider investments with regular cash flow, such

as dividend stocks or bonds, to ensure a steady source of income.

3. **Asset Liquidation:** Develop a plan for a smooth asset liquidation with the most minor tax fallout in times of extreme need.

Challenge 5: Passive Management Fatigue

1. **Automated Investments:** Using automated investing platforms and technologies simplifies portfolio management and reduces administrative responsibilities.

2. **Professional Management:** Consider engaging with a financial advisor or Robo-advisors to manage investment decisions on your behalf.

3. **Streamlined Portfolio:** Combine and arrange your investments for passive income for easier maintenance.

Challenge 6: Changing Life Circumstances

1. **Life Events:** Modify your passive income plans to consider significant life occurrences like marriage, parenthood, or retirement.

2. **Goal Reassessment:** Review and update your financial goals frequently to consider shifting priorities.

3. **Estate Planning:** Ensure that your passive income investments advance your estate planning objectives.

Conclusion

Finding answers to common issues is crucial to properly managing and growing your passive income account. You can prevent possible roadblocks by proactively addressing issues, including insufficient income, market volatility, tax complexity, liquidity constraints, passive management fatigue, and changing life circumstances. Investing in passive income is a long-term strategy; keep that in mind. You can continue to get closer to financial independence by keeping a positive attitude, being tough, and using an adaptive technique.

Conclusion

Chapter 10: Using Passive Income for Financial Independence

The final chapter of this comprehensive guide to passive income strategies tackles the ultimate goal: becoming financially independent. All of the knowledge, techniques, and insights you have acquired throughout the book are summed up in this chapter. We'll talk about the realistic steps, mental adjustments, and long-term planning required to reach the point where passive income allows you to live your desired lifestyle and pursue your interests, objectives, and aspirations. Follow along with us as we use the potential of passive income to reach complete financial freedom.

10.1: Your Personalized Passive Income Action Plan

Introduction to Your Personalized Passive Income Action Plan

As you read this book on passive income strategies, you learn much about various passive income streams, investment opportunities, and financial planning tactics. Now is the time to put this knowledge to work by creating a customized action plan that suits your unique financial goals and circumstances. This chapter will walk you through developing a unique passive income action plan.

Goal-setting and Self-Evaluation

1. **Financial Snapshot:** Take a close look at your current financial situation, including your earnings, outgoing costs, assets, liabilities, and savings.

2. **Clear Goals:** Outline your short- and long-term financial goals, such as when to retire early, your debt-reduction target, or the amount of passive income you hope to earn.

3. **Risk Tolerance:** Evaluate your comfort level with various investment

and income strategies by taking a risk tolerance test.

Identifying Passive Income Streams

1. **Passive Income Sources:** Look over the many passive income options described in this book and select the ones that best suit your interests and objectives.

2. **Diversification:** Consider varying your passive income sources to reduce risk and increase stability.

3. **Leveraging Strengths:** Look into new and personally fulfilling passive income opportunities using your skills, knowledge, and hobbies.

Creating a Timeline

1. **Short-Term Objectives:** Identify manageable short-term objectives, such as starting a side business or building an emergency fund.

2. **Medium-Term Milestones:** Define intermediate objectives, such as acquiring an investment property or quickly achieving a specific passive income objective.

3. **Long-Term Vision:** Outline your long-term financial objectives, including your projected retirement age or level of financial independence.

Allocation of assets and investment strategy

1. **Asset Allocation:** Considering your risk tolerance and financial goals, decide how to appropriately distribute your assets among different investment types.

2. **Investment Selection:** Based on your chosen passive income sources, select specific investments, such as dividend stocks, real estate, bonds, or a combination.

3. **Investment Horizon:** Consider how long you intend to hold your investments. Some passive income sources may pay out more quickly

than others.

Creating a budget and managing expenses

1. **Budget Creation:** Lay out a detailed spending plan that allocates your income between savings, investments, and essentials while allowing for discretionary spending.

2. **Expense Reduction:** Look for areas where you may reduce unnecessary spending and spend the money you save on investments that will produce passive income.

3. **Emergency Fund:** As a high priority, establish and manage an emergency fund to handle unanticipated financial setbacks without sacrificing your plans for passive income.

Monitoring and Adjustment

1. **Regular Review:** Commit to assessing your passive income action plan and tracking your progress toward your goals.

2. **Flexibility:** Be prepared to adapt your strategy as circumstances change, whether due to altering financial priorities, market conditions, or life events like events.

3. **Professional Guidance:** Consider seeking the advice of financial counselors or investment specialists to ensure that your plan stays on course and meets your goals.

Conclusion

Your passive income action plan is a dynamic document that evolves as you get closer to financial independence. By conducting a self-evaluation, setting precise goals, finding passive income sources, creating a timetable, devising an asset allocation strategy, controlling your budget, and committing to regular monitoring and adjustment, you'll be well on your way to attaining your financial goals. Accepting financial independence with passive income requires dedication, restraint, and a long-term perspective. You can achieve your financial goals if you have a solid plan and perseverance.

In the final section of this chapter, we'll provide some parting thoughts and encouragement as you start your road toward financial freedom.

Appendices

10.1.A: Resources and Tools for Passive Income

To create a successful passive income portfolio, you need more than just knowledge and strategy; you also need access to the resources and tools you'll need to manage your investments effectively. In this section, we'll look at the essential tools and supplies to support you toward achieving financial independence through passive income.

1. Financial Literacy and Education

- **Books and Publications:** Read reputable books, magazines, and financial publications to obtain a deeper grasp of passive income strategies, investment principles, and financial planning.

- **Online Courses:** Enroll in online courses or seminars offered by financial institutions and experts to deepen your awareness of specific passive income streams.

2. Investment Platforms and Accounts

- **Brokerage Accounts:** Open a brokerage account with a trustworthy website to invest in stocks, bonds, and ETFs.

- **Real Estate Platforms:** Look at online real estate investing websites that offer access to REIT or real estate crowdfunding.

- **Peer-to-Peer Lending Platforms:** Join a network of peer-to-peer lenders to benefit from chances for borrowing and lending.

3. Financial Analysis Tools

- **Investment Calculators:** Use investment calculators to analyze risk and potential returns and anticipate future income from your investments.

- **Portfolio Management Software:** Monitoring your asset allocation and investment performance using portfolio management software.

4. Market Research and Data Sources

- **Financial News Websites:** Keep up with market movements, economic news, and investment opportunities by visiting these websites.

- **Market Data Providers:** Access market statistics, stock quotes, and historical price data from reliable sources to assist you in making educated investment decisions.

5. Online forums and communities

- **Investor Communities:** Take part in online forums and groups to network with other investors, share experiences, and pick up tips on generating passive income.

- **Social Media Groups:** Join social media forums and groups dedicated to passive income so you can ask questions and receive help from others.

6. Financials Professionals and Advisors

- **Certified Financial Planners (CFPs):** Speak with CFPs specializing in passive income solutions for tailored advice and guidance.

- **Tax Advisors:** Consult a tax professional to assist you in maximizing your tax strategy, particularly for complex topics like dividend income or real estate.

7. Apps and Tools for Passive Income

- **Budgeting Apps:** Use budgeting apps to keep track of your earnings, outgoing costs, and savings so you may put more money into investments that will yield passive income.

- **Investment Apps:** Research investment applications that provide rapid access to various investment opportunities and allow you to manage your portfolio while on the road.

8. Educational Websites and Platforms

- **Online Forums and Communities:** Participate in online forums and communities with talks about investing, passive income, and financial education.

- **Educational Websites:** Visit educational platforms and websites that offer free resources, articles, and courses on topics relating to passive income.

9. Legal and Regulatory Resources

- **Government Websites:** Check out the official websites of your government to learn about the laws governing investments, taxes, and estate planning as they relate to passive income.

10. Newsletters and Email Subscriptions

- **Financial Newsletters:** To receive regular market information, investing guidance, and insights, subscribe to newsletters from financial analysts and professionals.

- **Email Alerts:** Set up email alerts for your investments to be notified of noteworthy events or changes that may impact your portfolio.

11. Networking Events and Seminars

- **Local Meetups:** Attend local passive income and investment networking events and gatherings to connect with like-minded individuals.

- **Investment Seminars:** Attend investment conferences and seminars to gain knowledge from pros in the field.

12. Legal Documents and Contracts

- **Legal Templates:** For leasing agreements, partnership agreements, and other passive income-related legal documents, use legal templates and contracts to ensure clarity and protection.

13. Economic Indicators and Reports

- **Government Reports:** Access government-produced economic reports and indicators to evaluate the status of the economy and find potential investment possibilities.

14. Resources for Risk Management and Insurance

- **Insurance Providers:** Speak with insurance providers to secure the required liability insurance, property insurance, and other forms of protection for your investments.

15. Online Investment Platforms

- **Robo-Advisors:** Robo-advisors are computerized portfolio managers that can provide investment recommendations based on your goals and risk tolerance. Consider using one of these online investment platforms.

16. Educational Institutions and Workshops

- **University Courses:** Research the online and in-person courses on investment and passive income that universities and other educational institutions provide.

With access to these tools and resources, you are better equipped to manage your investments, comprehend the complexity of passive income, and make wise choices.

10.1.B: Glossary of Terms Related to Passive Income

It takes a broad understanding of financial terms and concepts to navigate the realm of passive income. We've compiled a thorough dictionary of terms related to passive income to help you. Use this glossary as a resource to ensure you understand the terms connected with investments and passive income schemes.

Glossary of Terms for Passive Income

PASSIVE INCOME STRATEGIES FOR FINANCIAL INDEPENDENCE

1. Passive Income:

- **Definition:** Income obtained from sources over which you have only indirect or no control over day-to-day activities, such as investments, rental properties, dividends, interest, or royalties.

2. Asset Allocation:

- **Definition:** This refers to dividing investments across various asset classes, like stocks, bonds, real estate, and cash, to lower risk and achieve specific financial goals.

3. Diversification:

- **Definition:** Spreading investments over various assets or investment types to reduce risk and avoid concentration in a single investment.

4. Yield:

- **Definition:** The return on investment, typically expressed as a percentage, indicating how much income was generated relative to the investment's cost.

5. Dividend:

- **Definition:** Term used to denote a portion of a company's earnings distributed to shareholders, typically paid in cash or more stock.

6. Real Estate Investment Trust (REIT):

- **Definition:** An entity that owns or provides financing for income-producing real estate, allowing investors to participate in the real estate market without owning any real estate.

7. Capital Gains:

- **Definition:** The money made when an asset, like stocks or real estate, is sold for more than it was originally worth.

8. Passive Income Stream:

- **Definition:** A specific source of passive income, such as bond interest, rent on a property, or stock dividends.

9. Rental Property:

- **Definition:** Real estate that receives income from tenant rent payments.

10. Annuity:

- **Definition:** A financial product with repeating payments; frequently used as a source of assurance for retirement income.

11. Peer-to-Peer Lending:

- **Definition:** Peer-to-peer lending is an online service that connects people who are prepared to lend money to others who need it in exchange for interest payments.

12. Compound Interest:

- **Definition:** Earning interest on the initial principal and the accumulated interest from prior periods, causing an investment to increase exponentially.

13. Tax-Advantaged Accounts:

- **Definition:** Tax-advantaged accounts (TAAs) are financial accounts, such as IRAs and 401(k)s, that offer tax benefits and incentives to encourage retirement savings.

14. Dollar-Cost Averaging:

- **Definition:** A systematic investment approach in which an investor, regardless of market conditions, makes regular fixed-dollar purchases of an investment.

15. Robo-Advisor:

- **Definition:** Robo-advisors are algorithm-driven, automated investment platforms that manage clients' portfolios and provide investment advice per their risk tolerance and financial goals.

16. Emergency Fund:

- **Definition:** A savings account created to deal with unanticipated expenses or financial emergencies, ensuring financial security in tough times.

17. Asset Protection:

- **Definition:** Asset protection is the process of trying to shield assets from various threats, such as lawsuits, legal obligations, and creditors.

18. Estate Planning:

- **Definition:** Estate planning is the process of choosing how one's possessions and funds will be dispersed after death; it typically entails wills, trusts, and inheritance plans.

19. Financial Independence:

- **Definition:** Defined as having enough passive income to cover living expenses and the capacity to achieve financial goals without relying on a regular job.

20. Passive Management:

- **Definition:** Passive management, often associated with index funds or passive income methods, is a type of investment that requires little to no active involvement or decision-making on the part of the investor.

By giving you a fundamental grasp of the terms used in passive income, these definitions equip you to communicate with financial professionals, make sensible investment decisions, and navigate the complexity of the passive income landscape.

10.1.C: Recommended Reading List

Reading is one of the best ways to learn about and understand passive income strategies. This reading list covers various topics on personal finance, investing, financial independence, and passive income. Whether you're an experienced investor or a newbie, these tools can provide informative guidance on your path to financial freedom.

Recommended Reading List

1. "Rich Dad Poor Dad" by Robert Kiyosaki:

- **Description:** This famous text covers the concepts of financial education, passive income from real estate, and entrepreneurship, in addition to challenging traditional wealth notions.

2. "The Millionaire Next Door" by Thomas J. Stanley and William D. Danko:

- **Description:** Based on data, this article examines the habits and way of life of self-made millionaires and emphasizes the importance of being frugal, conserving money, and making smart investments.

3. "The Four Hour Workweek" by Timothy Ferriss:

- **Description:** Timothy Ferriss teaches how to become financially independent by automating revenue sources and building a life that gives more flexibility and adventure.

4. "The Bogleheads' Guide to Investing" by Taylor Larimore, Mel Lindauer, and Michael LeBoeuf:

- **Description:** This article provides a straightforward approach to passive investing using reasonably priced index funds, focusing on long-term wealth creation and risk control.

5. "The Book on Rental Property Investing" by Brandon Turner:

- **Description:** This book covers a lot of things, from finding, financing, and maintaining rental properties.

6. "Your Money or Your Life" by Vicki Robin and Joe Dominguez:

- **Description:** This is a comprehensive guide to altering your relationship with money, achieving financial independence, reducing expenses, and making wise investments.

7. "The Total Money Makeover" by Dave Ramsey:

- **Description:** provides a step-by-step plan for paying off debt, creating an emergency fund, and laying the foundation for investing and passive income.

8. "The Little Book of Common Sense Investing" by John C. Bogle:

- **Description:** John Bogle, who founded Vanguard, advocates a passive investment approach employing index funds and emphasizes the importance of simplicity and low fees.

9. "Cashflow Quadrant" by Robert Kiyosaki:

- **Description:** This book, a follow-up to "Rich Dad Poor Dad," covers the four revenue-generating quadrants and how to transition from an employee to a business owner and investor.

10. "The Simple Path to Wealth" by JL Collins:

- **Description:** An easy-to-follow guide to achieving financial independence and retiring early (FIRE) through index fund investment and enjoying a simple life.

11. "The Smart Passive Income Online Business and Blogging Podcast" (Podcast) by Pat Flynn:

- **Description:** This podcast features interviews with successful entrepreneurs and thought leaders in passive income, offering motivation and informative information.

12. "BiggerPockets" (Online Community and Podcast):

- **Description:** BiggerPockets is a fantastic website and podcast about real estate investing and achieving financial independence through real estate.

13. "Investopedia" (Website):

- **Description:** Investopedia is a comprehensive online resource that provides information on various financial and passive income possibilities through articles, videos, and how-to guides.

14. "Mr. Money Mustache" (Blog and Community):

- **Description:** A well-known site that explores achieving financial independence and retiring early through frugality, prudent investing, and lifestyle optimization.

These recommended readings cover various perspectives and strategies for achieving financial independence and developing passive income sources. Whether you are interested in real estate, stock market, business, or personal finance, these tools are valuable allies on your journey to financial freedom. Remember that self-education and continuous learning are essential to a successful passive income strategy.

ABOUT THE AUTHOR

Daniel Waweru is an accounting specialist with an exceptional Bachelor of Commerce in Accounting. He holds the CPAK and is a full member of the Institute of Certified Public Accountants of Kenya (ICPAK).

Daniel Waweru has worked at Saccos, audit firms, accounting colleges, and other industries, where he gained expertise in financial management, accounting, and auditing. Daniel Waweru has further contributed to the finance industry's educational landscape by lecturing at accounting colleges.

"Passive Income Strategies for Financial Independence" is based on his broad experience and proficiency in accounting and finance. Daniel Waweru is committed to giving readers the skills and information to become financially independent through passive income.